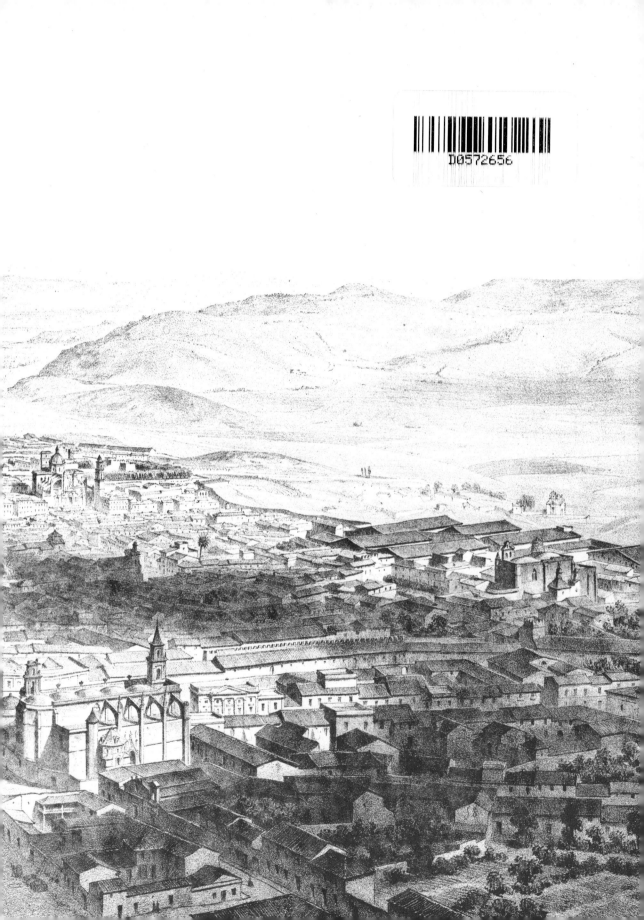

Sherry

AND THE SHERRY BODEGAS

Sherry
AND THE SHERRY BODEGAS

Jan Read

Sotheby's Publications

Frontispiece:
Sherry solera in one of Harvey's bodegas

Endpapers:
Bird's-eye view of Jerez (from L'Espagne à vol d'oiseau,
Paris, 1830)

First published 1988 for Sotheby's Publications
by Philip Wilson Publishers Ltd
26 Litchfield Street London WC2H 9NJ

Available to the USA Book Trade from
Sotheby's Publications
Harper & Row, Publishers, Inc
10 East 53rd Street New York NY 10022 USA

Exclusive distribution to the USA Wine Trade:
THE WINE APPRECIATION GUILD
155 Connecticut Street San Francisco
California 94107 USA
(415) 566-3532

ISBN 0 85667 349 8
LCC 88-060434

Designed by Mavis Henley

Printed by BAS Printers Limited,
Over Wallop, Hampshire and
bound by WBC Bookbinders Ltd,
Maesteg, Mid Glamorgan

Contents

Contents

Contents

Acknowledgements

I should first like to thank Mr Graham Hines and Mr Bryan Buckingham of the Sherry Institute in London and D. Bartolomé Vergara Vergara and D. Luís Bretón of the Asociación de Criadores Exportadores de Sherry, S.A., who made possible and arranged the numerous visits to Jerez on which the book is based.

Among the very many *bodegueros*, oenologists and staff at the sherry houses who have welcomed me and my wife over the years and taught me what I know about sherry are: Dr Fernando García-Delgado Bel of the Consejo Regulador; D. Mauricio González Gordon, D. Gabriel González Gilbey and Dr Justo Casas of González Byass, S.A.; D. José Ignacio Domecq, D. José Ignacio Domecq Jr and D. Manuel de Domecq Zurita of Pedro Domecq, S.A.; D. Manuel de Ysasi Díaz of Garvey, S.A.; D. Diego Ferguson and D. Ignacio López de Carrizosa Domecq of Harvey & Sons (España) Ltd; D. Juan M. López de Carrizosa Domecq of Croft Jerez, S.A.; D. Rafael Balao and D. Manuel Arcila Martín of Emilio Lustau, S.A.; D. Juan Pazos and D. Pepe Gil Caballero of Sandeman-Coprimar, S.A. and Mr John Lockwood, formerly of the firm; D. Miguel Valdespino of A. R. Valdespino, S.A.; D. Jaime González Gordon and D. Antonio Arias of Wisdom & Warter Ltd; D. Carlos del Río of Bodegas Internacionales, S.A.; D. Javier Hidalgo de Argueso of Vinícola Hidalgo, S.A.; D. Alfredo Campos Peña and D. Julián Pérez of Palomino & Vergara, S.A.; D. Enrique Valle Sevilla of Hijos de Rainera Pérez Marín, S.A.; D. Alfonso Lacave Ruíz-Tagle of Diez-Mérito, S.A.; D. Tomás Osborne Domecq, D. Tomás Osborne Gamero-Civico, D. Eligio Pastor Nimo and Mr Jan Pettersen of Osborne y Cia; D. Luís Caballero of Luís Caballero, S.A.; Mr Pieter van Panhuys of José de la Cuesta, S.L.; D. Alfonso Barón Rojas-Marcos and D. Gabriel Raya of Antonio Barbadillo, S.A.; D. José Munilla Murillo of Williams & Humbert Ltd and formerly of Duff Gordon & Co.; D. Fernando Gago and D. Fernando García-Borreguero of Fernando A. de Terry, S.A. I recall with gratitude that I was first received at a sherry bodega by D. Antonio Cuvillo, whose firm, maker of excellent wines, alas, no longer exists. I remember, too, in the days of RUMASA, the very hospitable reception at Zoilo Ruíz-Mateos, S.A. at the hands of D. Zoilo Ruíz-Mateos and his then Director of Public Relations,

Srta Fátima Ruíz-Lasaleta.

The chapter on the cuisine of the sherry region has been prepared with the help of Lalo Grosso de Macpherson, *Cocinera del Rey* ('Royal Cook') and *Cocinera del Jerez.*

Warm thanks go to my wife's cousin Don Antonio ('Toto') León y Manjón of the Marqués del Real Tesoro, a fund of information and the most hospitable of hosts at his house in Jerez and *finca* in the sierra, who must know every single member of the sherry community.

Over the years the British representatives of the sherry firms have been most helpful, among them: Mr Charles Gordon, Mr David Palengat and Mr Jeffrey Fredericks of Luis Gordon & Sons; D. Francisco Valencia of González Byass (UK) Ltd; and D. Alejandro Cassinello and Mr John Hunt of La Riva.

Nobody who embarks on a book about sherry could do so without acknowledging a debt of gratitude to two authors, whose books remain a model for anyone temerarious enough to approach the subject. I refer, of course, to *Sherry, the Noble Wine* by Manuel M. González Gordon, Marqués de Bonanza, and *Sherry* by Julian Jeffs, now in its third edition. I am grateful, too, to that aficionado of Spanish wines in the United States, Mr Gerry Dawes, for the excerpt from an article in *The New York Wine Cellar.*

Finally, I wish to thank my wife, Maite Manjón, who accompanied me on most of my visits to Jerez, for contributing the chapter on cuisine, helping with the tasting notes and stepping in when my Spanish failed me.

Introduction

'Sherry,' Richard Ford once wrote, 'is a foreign wine, and made and drunk by foreigners' – meaning, of course, the British. If his comment is chauvinistic, it nevertheless reflects the family ties between Britain and Jerez, and as in the best conducted of families there have been ups and downs in the relationship. In 1979 sherry was riding high; recently there has been some decline in its popularity, but it will always remain one of the most lively and various of wines, of which different styles may be drunk with pleasure before, during and after a meal.

There has not been a new book on sherry, apart from the revised editions of Julian Jeffs' admirable *Sherry*, for the last quarter of a century. During this period Jerez de la Frontera has probably seen more change, technological and in the structure of the trade, than at any other period of its history, hence, as a devotee and frequent visitor, my own interest.

A few years ago the sherry industry faced a crisis. The Spanish conglomerate RUMASA, which had gained control of some 35 per cent of the bodegas, had been cutting corners and dumping stocks and was finally expropriated by the Spanish government. In Spain itself, never a large market for sherry outside its native Andalucía, it was becoming more chic to drink Scotch whisky. And in Britain, where we have traditionally drunk more sherry than the rest of the world put together, television advertisements were persuading the young that it was a great deal more glamorous and more fun to drink vermouth.

The producers took stock and embarked on a four-year plan. One thing for which RUMASA must be given credit was the introduction of modern technology. This has since proceeded apace with the installation of modern presses and temperature-controlled fermentation in stainless steel tanks, without prejudice to the age-long tradition of maturing the wine in *solera* or to its quality – indeed the quality and freshness of *fino* has probably improved. One outcome has been the reduction of the labour force to economic levels – at one of the largest bodegas, which was threatened with bankruptcy because of huge labour costs, from 1,500 to some 350. Other measures have included stricter quality control, the fixing of sensible minimum prices, a reduction in the total vineyard area and vigorous advertising campaigns both at home and abroad.

Spain's entry into the EEC does not as yet appear to have brought Jerez any particular benefits, indeed it has resulted in a steep rise in the cost of alcohol used for fortification, so adding to the producers' overheads. Apart from another new entrant, Portugal, the members of the Community do not produce fortified wines in significant amount and are almost exclusively interested in light wines. Jerez's fifty-year-old *denominación de origen* is not even to be recognised nor the name 'sherry' adequately protected. What particularly rankles is the ten-year moratorium allowing for the continued use of the name 'British Sherry' for a product which the Jerezanos claim in no recognisable way resembles the orignal. The forthright Luís Caballero reported to me that he had roundly said to Felipe González, the Spanish Prime Minister; 'You are using Jerez as a pawn to obtain rights on fishing and agriculture.'

Jerez has weathered many storms in its centuries' long history, from Sir Francis Drake's rape of the butts to the disastrous slump of the early 1900s, when Edward VII sold a surplus of 60,000 bottles from the royal cellars. Never a favourite in the United States – though it appears that shipments of *almacenista* sherry are presently selling out on the Eastern seaboard as soon as they are landed – it has elsewhere survived the dry martini or gin sling, and a chilled glass of *fino* (or champagne) remains the best apéritif before a meal at which other wines are to be drunk. All sherry is remarkable value considering the time and skill which go into its making, and the cost of the choicest old *amontillado, palo cortado, oloroso* or *almacenista* sherry is nowhere near that of one of the better vintage clarets.

CHAPTER 1

The Sherry Region

The sherry region, an area of low, rolling hills of sunbaked white clay densely carpeted with dark green vines, extends for some 50 kilometres (30 miles) northwards of Cádiz in the extreme south of Andalucía towards Seville. Just beyond its western boundary, the estuary of the River Guadalquivir, lies the Coto Doñana, one of the last great nature reserves in Europe, and to the east, beyond the River Guadalete and the cliff-top Moorish town of Arcos de la Frontera, the wooded and mountainous Serranía de Ronda and in its fastnesses Grazalema, 'plastered', as Richard Ford once wrote, 'like a martlet nest on the rocky hill'. It was here during the Peninsular War that 'the inhabitants, smugglers and robbers, beat back a whole division of the French, who compared it to a land Gibraltar.' The whole area is one of the most scenic and least spoilt in Spain and well worth visiting quite apart from the attractions of the sherry towns of Jerez de la Frontera, Puerto de Santa María and Sanlúcar de Barrameda.

The quickest way to reach it is either to fly direct to Seville and to hire a car at the airport or to take a taxi to Jerez, about an hour-and-half's drive south down the *autopista* to Cádiz. Alternatively, one may fly to Madrid and then proceed by an internal Aviaco flight to Jerez, where there is a small airport – until recently it was possible to sit in

1 *House in the Barrio de Santa Cruz, Seville*

13

the open air with a glass of *fino* within two minutes' walk of the plane in which one was about to take off. For railway buffs there is the Talgo from Madrid to Cádiz, a luxury train which stops at Jerez, making the journey in some seven hours, which go by fast enough thanks to the variegated scenery and excellent meals and service. More recently, RENFE, the nationalised Spanish railway, has inaugurated the Andalucía Express, a train along the lines of the Orient Express with lovingly restored period Pullman, sleeping and saloon cars, making a five-day tour of Andalucía with a day's stopover in Jerez and a visit to the bodegas.

Seville and Cádiz at either end of the *autopista* which bisects the vineyards both deserve extended visits, but are very different in character. The heart of Seville is the great gothic cathedral and La Giralda, once the minaret of the mosque which it replaced. Within a stone's throw are the Moorish Alcázar with its splendid coloured tiles and gardens cool with running water, and the Barrio de Santa Cruz, the old Jewish quarter, an intricate network of narrow streets opening

2 The esplanade, Cádiz

on to small, unsuspected tree-lined squares and secret patios. The city is the undoubted capital of Andalucía; it houses the Archives of the Indies and, connected to the sea by the River Guadalquivir, was the hub of the colonial trade with South America. Across the river is Triana, famous for its gypsies, flamenco and Easter processions.

Cádiz, too, has its narrow streets providing shade from the beating Andalucían sun, but the overriding impression of this great southern seaport is of glittering white buildings, domed churches, wide squares and an encircling promenade with views across shimmering blue water and towards the coast of Africa, hazy on the horizon. In the past Cádiz was more of a sherry town than it is now, with important firms maintaining their offices and bodegas there before they moved to Jerez de la Frontera and Puerto de Santa María in the early nineteenth century. It remains the principal port for shipping sherry.

Foremost of the sherry towns is, of course, Jerez de la Frontera. It is a place of contrasts, now ringed with modern roads and high rise apartment blocks; driving from the airport down the wide but rather characterless main avenue into the centre, one would not suspect that around the old Moorish fortress or *alcázar*, flanked in spring with a line of sky-blue jacaranda trees, there is a haven of quiet, up-and-down streets, small squares and white-washed houses splashed with geraniums. But the greatest attraction of Jerez is the sherry bodegas themselves, sited in their scores inside the town and around it, sometimes discreetly hidden by a high wall, sometimes looming cathedral-like or in Richard Ford's phrase 'like the pent-houses under which men-of-war are built at Chatham' and often, like Oxford colleges, surrounded by spacious decorative gardens.

The pleasantest times to visit Jerez are in May, before the breathless summer heat descends, or in the afterglow of late October, with the rolling vineyards russet-coloured in the low sun. The town is at its liveliest during the horsefair in late April or early May when the Arab thoroughbreds are paraded, there are dressage competitions and the old carriages drawn by splendidly harnessed and decorated teams of horses are brought out from the stables of the bodegas, and again during the Fiesta de la Vendimia (harvest festival) in early September. Each year this festival is dedicated to one of the different countries to which sherry is exported and is climaxed by a procession through the streets, headed by the Queen of the Vintage accompanied by her maids of honour and the ritual pressing and blessing of the first grapes on the steps of the Collegiate Church. The bells ring out and the sky is suddenly alive with the whir of hundreds of doves released to carry the message of the new vintage.

3 *Moorish street in Arcos de la Frontera*

In the words of sherry's own poet, Manuel Barbadillo:

Paloma sin vasallaje,
yo impregno el mundo de olor,
de éste Jerez ya hecho flor,
brindis, guitarra y mensaje

(Free-flying dove, carrying with it
the heady smell of new wine and a toast
and music from Jerez)

At times other than the Fiesta and the annual holidays in August, the bodegas welcome visitors. No prior notice is necessary at the larger concerns, such as González Byass, Pedro Domecq and Williams & Humbert, where there are English-speaking guides and the visit ends with a tasting of different styles of sherry, properly served in *copitas*, the *fino* from chilled half-bottles. Other firms, such as Sandeman, require notice, and with the smaller it is always advisable to write or telephone beforehand and, if possible, to come armed with a letter from someone in the trade.

The second of the sherry townships, Puerto de Santa María, lies on the coast between Jerez and Cádiz, and was once the main port for the shipment of sherry, but its Trocadero mole long since fell into disuse and is being transformed into an exclusive leisure centre and yachting marina. The centre of the town preserves its old character, its handsome streets lined by houses with heavy ornamental grilles on the windows. It boasts one of the largest and most ornate bull-rings in Spain, constructed by the sherry family of Osborne; and another sherry family, that of Caballero, has recently restored the Moorish castle of San Marcos, once a seat of the Dukes of Medinaceli. The sea airs of Puerto de Santa María greatly benefit the making of *fino*; a number of the big firms from Jerez de la Frontera maintain bodegas in the Puerto for the purpose, and it is also the headquarters of a number of other large firms. Some of its bodegas, notably those of Terry and Osborne, with their enchanting tree-lined patios and buildings hung with purple bougainvillaea, are architecturally interesting, as is the old building of John William Burdon (now the stables for Terry's famous Carthusian horses) with its imposing stone pediment.

Apart from being a sherry centre, Puerto de Santa María is a flourishing seaside resort with holiday hotels and a casino and aquapark just outside it.

Sanlúcar de Barrameda, at the mouth of the River Guadalquivir, from which Columbus sailed on his third voyage to America, is even more famous for its sea breezes than Puerto de Santa María, and they are reputedly responsible for its special style of sherry, the light, dry and salty *manzanilla*, made there and there alone. It is fronted by a long beach of fine sand, and across the water, with ships bound to and from Seville passing regularly by, is the low shoreline of Las Marismas and the nature reserve of the Coto Doñana, frequented by great flocks of migratory birds on their way between Africa and Europe, and the permanent home of the rare Spanish eagle and other birds and animals of all sorts. Tantalisingly near, there is no ferry except at the time of the Festival of El Rocío in June, and to reach it one must cross the river upstream at Seville.

There is a fine church in Sanlúcar, that of Santa María de la O, and the town is surmounted by the old castle of the Dukes of Medina Sidonia. The former bishop's palace is now the headquarters of the largest of its sherry firms, Barbadillo. There were at one time many more small bodegas than there are now, some of them being attached to the old baronial houses. The town remains a thriving centre for the production of *manzanilla* and other sherries.

A car (which may be hired on the spot at Seville airport) is of course useful for exploring the area. When driving from Seville, the best way to get an impression of the vineyards is to branch off the motorway at Las Cabezas, about half-way to Jerez, and follow the by-road through Lebrija and Trebujana and the famous vineyards of Macharnudo and Carrascal. It is, however, possible to see a great deal by taking taxis to the bodegas and making use of the regular electric trains from Jerez into the centre of Cádiz, stopping en route at Puerto de Santa María.

4 The white walls of Andalucía

5 Jerezana *riding one of the famous Carthusian horses*

HOTELS
(For restaurants see Chapter 8)

Arcos de la Frontera
Parador Nacional Casa del Corregidor***
Plaza de España; tel. 70 05 00.
32 kilometres (20 miles) east of Jerez, the *parador* is magnificently perched on a cliff above the River Guadalete in this old Moorish town. Some authentic regional dishes and a good house wine from Chiclana.

Cádiz
Hotel Atlántico****
Duque de Nájera, 9; tel. 21 23 01.
Recently reconstructed, this remains the only hotel in the *parador* network. It overlooks the sea near the southernmost tip of Cádiz and has recently won awards for its cooking.

Jerez de la Frontera
Hotel Jerez*****
Avenida Alcalde Alvaro Domecq, 41; tel. 30 06 00.
There is a shortage of accommodation in Jerez, especially at festival times, and reservations should be made well in advance. New hotels have been built, but this, with its large garden and swimming pool, remains the most attractive.

Hotel Royal Sherry Park****
Avenida Alcalde Alvaro Domecq, 11 bis; tel. 30 30 11.
Large new hotel in spacious garden.

Hotel Avenida Jerez***
Avenida Alcalde Alvaro Domecq, 8; tel. 34 74 11.

Puerto de Santa María
Meliá El Caballo Blanco***
Crtra de Cádiz, 2·5 kilometres; tel. 86 37 45.
A resort hotel with bungalows in a pleasant garden.

Puertobahía***
Playa. S., 3·5 kilometres; tel. 86 27 21.
Large seaside hotel on the beach.

Sanlúcar de Barrameda
Until very recently Sanlúcar could offer no accommodation of good standard. There are now four establishments, all of them small but with modern comforts in meticulously converted old houses.

Palacio Ducal
Plaza de los Condes de Niebla; tel. 36 01 61.
This defies classification, since there are simply three rooms in a beautifully restored wing of the historic ducal palace made available to visitors by the Duquesa de Medina Sidonia.

La Posada de Palacio**
Plaza de los Condes de Niebla
Tiled patio, antique furniture, literary and artistic clientele, to cater for whose desire for tranquillity there is *no* telephone.

Hotel Los Helechos**
Plaza Madre de Dios, 9; tel. 36 14 41.

*Hotel Tartaneros***
Tartaneros, 8; tel. 36 35 50.

Seville

There are dozens of comfortable hotels in Seville – consult the current edition of the red Michelin. The largest, most famous and most expensive, the *Alfonso XIII*, built in Moorish style and conveniently close to the Cathedral and centre, is being renovated by its new owners; in the meantime service and cuisine are patchy.

6 *The sherry region*

Map labels: TREBUJENA, SANLÚCAR DE BARRAMEDA, CHIPIONA, R. Guadalquivir, Miraflores, Torrebreba, Madroñales, Tehigo, Añina, Macharnudo, Carrascal, Balbaina, Los Tercios, JEREZ DE LA FRONTERA, ARCOS DE LA FRONTERA, R. Guadalete, ROTA, PUERTO DE SANTA MARIA, CADIZ, PUERTO REAL, SAN FERNANDO, CHICLANA DE LA FRONTERA, Santi Petri, ATLANTIC OCEAN, SPAIN, Jerez

Legend:
- Clays and sands
- Chalky soils (*albarizas*)
- Railways
- Major roads

CHAPTER 2

The History

Xerez de la Frontera or Jerez, from which sherry takes its name,

> rises amid vine-clad slopes, with its white-washed Moorish towers, blue domed *Colegiata*, and huge *Bodegas*, or wine stores, looking like pent-houses for men-of-war at Chatham. It is supposed by some to be the ancient [Roman] Asta regia Caesariana . . . Xerez is a straggling, ill-built, ill-drained, Moorish city, with a popn. of 32,000. Part of the original walls and gates remain in the old town: the suburbs are more regular, and here the wealthy wine-merchants reside. Xerez was taken from the Moors in 1264, by Alonzo the learned. The Alcazar, near the public walk is very perfect . . . The *Colegiata* is vile churrigueresque; the architect did not by accident stumble on one sound rule, or deviate into the commonest sense . . .

So Richard Ford, writing his his *Handbook for Spain* of 1845 on the appearance and origins of Jerez. Although there has since been much speculation about the early history of the town, nothing very definite has emerged, except that it was probably founded by the Phoenicians, and that Greeks, Carthaginians, Romans, Goths and Vandals all passed this way. The conclusion reached by Manuel González Gordon in his scholarly *Sherry, The Noble Wine* is: 'What can more positively be asserted is that the town of Jerez is the *Sherrish* of the Moors, and that it is mainly of Arab origin' and that 'The period of Moorish–Arab domination which gave Jerez its present name is the most interesting of all. From it stem the legacy of the buildings and monuments, the popular music and customs of the district and indeed the temperament

7 *Bird's-eye view of Jerez (from* L'Espagne à vol d'oiseau, *Paris, 1830)*

8 *Approaching Jerez from Cádiz: an early view*

of its people, endowed as they are with their own very distinctive characteristics.'

Wine had been exported in large quantity to Rome from the province of Betica (the south-west of Andalucía) from very early times, and there are amphorae in Roman museums dating from the year AD 31 labelled *Vinum Digatanum*, which perhaps contained a forerunner of the present-day sherry. During the long years of Moorish occupation from 711 to 1264, wine-making was discouraged because of the Koranic ban on alcoholic drinks and vines were grown principally for raisins. Nevertheless wine continued to be made and sold by the Christian Mozarabs and was drunk even by the emirs and caliphs of al-Andalus, and especially during the later period, after the break-up of the Cordoban caliphate, by the rulers of the *taifas* into which it disintegrated. So al-Mu'tamid (1040–95), the poet king of Seville, could write:

> As I was passing by
> A vine, its tendrils tugged my sleeve,
> 'Do you design,' said I,
> 'My body so to grieve?'
>
> 'Why do you pass,' the vine
> Replied, 'and never greeting make?
> It took this blood of mine
> Your thirsting bones to slake.'

After the reconquest of Jerez in 1264, Alfonso X granted lands to the knights, such as Fernán Yanez Palomino, forbear of the famous sherry family, who had helped him recapture the city. According to Francisco de Mesa Ginete's *Historia de Xerez*, forty councillors and knights were each allocated six *aranzadas* or about seven acres, half of it vineyard, and enjoined to plant the rest with young vines. Even at that time records show that there were many buildings in the town listed as *bodegas*.

Export of wine from Jerez to England probably began during the first half of the fourteenth century, if not even earlier, and reached more substantial proportions during the latter part of the fifteenth, when relations between the two countries, which have undergone such perennial vicissitudes, entered on a brief honeymoon during the reign

9 Jerez in the early nineteenth century

of Henry VII and the marriage of his son with Catherine of Aragon. When the Catholic Monarchs, Ferdinand and Isabel, expelled the Jews from Spain in 1492, they were succeeded in southern Spain by English, Breton and Genoese merchants – much the amalgam, less the Maltese, which makes up present-day Gibraltar. During the sixteenth century the British settled in force in Sanlúcar de Barrameda, where the Dukes of Medina Sidonia made special concessions to the effect that 'all persons, both Spanish and foreign, resident or non-resident, in the town, would be allowed to ship their *romania* [rumney] wines, or any other product of their properties, free of tax providing that they declared such products to be the produce of Jerez.' Julian Jeffs' *Sherry* contains a fascinating account of some of these early English merchants, including one Juan Esvique (surely a Spanish rendering of 'Esquire'), who tangled with the authorities, and of their troubles when Anglo–Spanish accord came to an end with Henry VIII's divorce of Catherine of Aragon and Sir Francis Drake's raids on the Spanish coast.

There is an odd story in a book by Diego Parada y Barreto, *Hombres ilustres de Jerez*, to the effect that in earlier life Drake had been a merchant in Jerez, but after a violent quarrel had shaken its dust off his feet and from then on knew no bounds in his hostility towards Spain. In 1587 he attacked Cádiz and made off with supplies intended for the Spanish Armada, including 2,900 pipes of sherry. Even more damaging to the Jerezanos was the commandeering of sherry and of empty sherry butts for storing water, by the Spanish admiral the Duke of Medina Sidonia in 1580 at the time of the war with Portugal and for the Armada.

At least Drake's seizure of the sherry butts resulted in the release on the English market of large amounts of sherry, or 'sack' as it was then known, just when it was becoming popular and was at its scarcest. In modern terms, the promotion was cheap at the price. Shakespeare, too, contributed to its growing popularity; Falstaff's encomium is well-known, but too good not to repeat:

> A good sherris-sack hath a twofold operation in it. It ascends me into the brain; dries me there all the foolish and dull and crudy vapours which environ it; makes it apprehensive, quick, forgetive, full of nimble, fiery, and delectable shapes; which deliver'd o'er to the voice, the tongue, which is the birth, becomes excellent wit. The second property of your excellent sherris is, the warming of the blood; which, before cold and settled, left the liver white and pale, which is the badge of pusillanimity and cowardice; but the sherris warms it and makes it course from the inwards to the parts extreme ... If I had a thousand sons, the first humane

10 *The eighteenth-century Palacio Domecq in Jerez*

principle I would teach them should be, to forswear thin potations, and to addict themselves to sack.

The derivation of this word has been debated at inordinate length, but it is virtually certain that it is from the Spanish verb *sacar*, to 'withdraw' or 'export', since it was also used for other fortified wines imported into England, such as Canary and Málaga.

By the middle of the seventeenth century, sherry was being widely drunk throughout Europe. It was made in small cellars and traded by forgotten merchants, and the first of the firms to survive until the

11 *Macharnudo Castle in the vineyards of Pedro Domecq (from an aquatint, c. 1830)*

present day and to evolve as a concern with large stocks of wine and spacious bodegas in which to mature it was that of J.M. Rivero, whose records date back to 1653. Its history and that of its famous 'C.Z.' brand is told in the section of this book on the bodegas.

The first firm of the very many to be founded by British immigrants was that of Rafael O'Neale, established in 1724 by Timothy O'Neale, a refugee from the troubles in Ireland; it survived as a small house selling fine wines until the early 1980s. A number of the present-day sherry concerns, among them some of the largest, started business during the eighteenth century. They include, in Jerez, Pedro Domecq, founded under the name of Juan Haurie in 1730; Luís G. Gordon (1754); La Riva (1776); Garvey (1780) and Sánchez Romate (1781). Duff Gordon (1768) first began business in Cádiz, soon moving to Puerto de Santa María and forming an Anglo–Scottish alliance with Osborne, founded by a Devonshireman in 1781. In Sanlúcar de Barrameda the oldest surviving firms are Delgado Zuleta (1719) and Hidalgo (1792). Details of these and all the present *Bodegas de Crianza y Expedición* (those which mature and ship sherry) will be found in the section on the bodegas.

It took Jerez many years to recover from the devastation caused by the Peninsular War and the French occupation of Spain, which finally came to an end in 1813. However, the early decades of the nineteenth century saw the emergence of two giants of the industry, when Pedro Domecq Lembeye took over the house of Haurie in 1822 and Manuel María González Angel, the founder of Gonzáles Byass, acquired his first bodega in 1833. The lion's share of exports (in 1844, a staggering 92

COMPARATIVE STATEMENT OF THE SHIPMENTS OF SHERRY WINES FOR 1843 & 1844.

LIST OF SHIPPERS. PORT ST. MARY'S.	1843. BUTTS.	1844. BUTTS.	LIST OF SHIPPERS. XEREZ.	1843. BUTTS.	1844. BUTTS.
Messrs. J. W. Burdon	1927	2015	Messrs. P. Garvey	1851	1658
J. M. Pico	1633	1410	P. Domecq	1809	2060
W. Oldham	1432	1947	Pemartin & Co.	1566	1809
M. M. Mora	1316	1513	Gordon & Co.	1448	1554
Diaz. Merello & Co.	1214	1171	Beigbeder & Co.	1358	1148
Perez. Bro's & Capdepon	1104	1017	J. Haurie Nephew	658	592
Duff. Gordon & Co.	1029	1017	Gonzales & Dubosc	638	1260
Vergara & Dickison	502	616	Ysasi & Co.	604	1010
A. R. Tagle	438	441	Bermudez & Co.	562	677
F. X. Harmony	421	443	D. de Goni	538	602
Allen. Morgan & Co.	325	347	P. L. Villegas	483	675
V. M. de la Portilla	257	280	Paul & Dastis	461	890
J. Gargollo	238	——	J. Domecq & Sons	419	534
F. Heald	232	322	Lacoste & Capdepon	394	407
J. A. Aramburn	210	125	Thomas Waters	317	329
Allnutts & Co.	195	——	P. A. Rivero & Sons	242	377
Widow de Victoria & Sons	187	300	S. Sierra	215	582
J. J. Iriarte	184	495	Ostman H y Urrutia	194	425
Urucla. Brothers & Co.	178	117	Quarles. Harris & Co.	104	——
R. P. Gasten	167	——	J. A. Agreda	——	212
G. Thuiller	139	——	P. R. Sorela	——	205
M. & F. TOSAR	124	330	24 Shippers under 100 Butts each	436	——
Gorman & Co.	119	112	21 Shippers under 100 butts each	——	502
A. Albertis	109	110			
M. Sevill	107	——			
Lacave & Echecopar	102	——			
T. M. Waters	101	——			
Tabrada & Portilla	——	549			
C. S. Campbell & Co.	——	391			
J. M. de Thovias	——	248			
H. Oncale y Saelizes	——	177			
J. Moustey & Co.	——	173			
Vidow de Echeverregaray	——	152			
32 Shippers under 100 Butts each	1026	——			
27 Shippers under 100 Butts each	——	840			
Butts	15016	16658	Butts	14297	17508

Recapitulation.

PORT ST. MARY'S. 1843 :—— Butts. 15016   PORT ST. MARY'S. 1844   Butts. 16658
XEREZ.   do. ..   14297——Total. 29313   XEREZ   do. ..   17508——Total. 34166
Increase in 1844. Butts. 4853

Distribution of Shipments in 1844.

	BUTTS.	BUTTS.		BUTTS.	BUTTS.
London	23140		Exeter	130	
Dublin	2157		Newcastle	124	31447
Liverpool	1759		Hamburgh	392	
Leith	1307		Vera Cruz	289	
Glasgow	642		Malta	241	
Gloster	549		New York	126	
Bristol	542		St. Petersburg	112	
Hull	420		Lima	111	
Cork	356		59 other Markets	1448	2719
Belfast	186				
Plymouth	135		Total		34166

per cent) went, as it has done ever since, to Great Britain, and numerous firms originated in the British agents of the shippers moving out to Cádiz and Jerez to take charge on the spot, and with clerks in their employ, such as John William Burdon or Alexander Williams, setting up on their own. One of the earliest and most important of these British merchants was the Scottish C.P. Gordon, who kept open house for visitors from home, entertaining Lord Byron in 1809, and whose son became British Vice-Consul in Jerez. The accompanying list of leading sherry houses and their shipments in 1843 and 1844 gives an idea of the British penetration of the business; and names, both British and Spanish, like F.X. Harmony, the Widows of Rd. Shiel and Victoria & Sons, Ysasi and Beigbeder, once leading shippers of their day and now almost forgotten, make nostalgic reading.

The shipment of wine from Jerez de la Frontera had always presented difficulties and it was formerly taken by ox-cart to El Portal on the River Guadalete and then downstream to Puerto de Santa María for trans-shipment. The problems only increased as trade boomed in the nineteenth century. In 1827 the famous George Stephenson visited Jerez to investigate the linking of Jerez to Puerto de

12 *The Sandeman topsail schooner, built in 1865*

13 *Puerto de Santa María in the mid-nineteenth century*

Santa María and Sanlúcar de Barrameda by rail, but the project came to nothing. It was not until 1854 that a railway (only the third in Spain) was opened between Jerez and Puerto de Santa María and the old Trocadero quay. This, with an urban system serving the bodegas, greatly eased the situation; but the Trocadero eventually fell into disrepair and has not been used since 1922, shipments now going by container from Cádiz or Algeciras. The practice of shipping in bottle rather than in butt first started with the firm of J. de Fuentes Parrilla (later taken over by Diez Hermanos, now Diez–Mérito) between 1871 and 1873.

It was at this time that the nineteenth-century sherry boom reached its peak with record shipments of 61,811 and 68,467 butts in 1872 and 1873, but within two decades the trade was to suffer a sharp set-back. In the first place this was caused by the onset of that disastrous plague of the wine, phylloxera.

Phylloxera first reached Spain in 1875, when it broke out in the vineyards of Lagar de la Indiana twelve miles outside Málaga, probably being introduced by plants sent from the south of France. It was hoped that the high mountains between Málaga and Jerez might prevent the spread of the insect, which attacks the roots of the vine, or again that it would not penetrate the compact *albariza* soil.

All proved to be wishful thinking. The plague spread like wildfire from Málaga to Lebrija in the north of the sherry region, soon engulfing the whole area and reaching Jerez on 21 July 1894. The usual remedies of spraying with insecticide and injecting carbon disulphide into the soil were tried, but the larger part of the vineyards in Jerez were ruined, and it soon became clear that the only solution was to grub up the existing vines and to replant with resistant American root-stocks, on to which the native varieties were grafted.

'Troubles come not single spies' and Jerez's misfortunes led to growing foreign competition from cheaper 'sherry'-type wines. The low quality of some of the wine shipped from Jerez itself was another cause of much reduced exports around the turn of the century, but the major factor was over-stocking in England, where sherry had fallen out of fashion, partly because of wrong-headed but sustained attacks by a Dr Thudichum, a Victorian health fanatic, on the innocent practice of 'plastering' (or dusting the grapes with a little gypsum to increase the acidity of the must and help fermentation).

The popularity of *manzanilla* does not seem to have been so much affected by the slump. According to Manuel Barbadillo the late nineteenth and early twentieth century was the golden era of the wine. At that time there were no less than 86 bodegas in Sanlúcar de Barrameda, and wine was stored in the basements of all the old houses, its fragrance wafting up to perfume the living quarters. *Manzanilla* was the toast of Spanish writers from Bécquer to Pérez Galdós and Quintero, and rejoiced in appropriately evocative feminine names – 'La Pastora', 'La Victoria', 'La Goya', 'La Gitana', 'La Guita', 'Soleá', 'Solear', 'Eva' and the rest (though 'Eva of the *finos*' was not at that time *quite* as profitable as its fame would suggest – in an untranslatable Andalucían phrase, *más el ruido que las nueces de la manzanilla*, or very roughly 'more talk than taste').

Sherry returned to fashion by the end of the First World War and exports reached a new peak of 1,500,000 hectolitres or the equivalent of 300,000 butts in 1979. By this time the practice of shipping sherry in butt for bottling in Britain, once more or less universal, had virtually been phased out. On the one hand, the very big-selling *finos* such as 'Tío Pepe' were being transported in nitrogen-capped containers and kept in cool nitrogen-capped tanks until bottled, since the shippers maintained that it reaches the customer fresher in this way than when despatched in bottle. An increasing amount of sherry, including all the fine old wines, is, however, now bottled at the bodega itself.

Important in the long run as were such technical innovations as this and the cloning of vines, the picking of the fruit into plastic baskets, the installation of modern presses instead of the crushing of the fruit with the traditional nail-studded *zapatos de pisar* and temperature-controlled fermentation in stainless steel, the industry was to be shaken by more dramatic events during the decades of the '60s and '70s and the shattering collapse on Thursday 24 February 1983 of a concern which had engulfed an estimated third to half of the sherry trade.

In 1944 Don Zoilo Ruíz-Mateos y Camacho, the much-respected Mayor of Rota and of a family one of whose forbears was the contentious Pope Pedro de Luna, bought a small bodega in Jerez housing three hundred butts of wine. The story proper begins in 1955 when his ambitious young son, José María, began writing letters to Harvey's of the famous 'Bristol Cream', asking to supply them with wine. The following year he persuaded them to buy fifty butts, and it was not long before he had signed them to an exclusive 99-year deal for supplying all their requirements of sherry. To fulfil this huge order he borrowed from the banks and began buying up bodegas. Beginning with the small family firm of A.R. Ruiz in 1959, he was to swallow up Pemartín, Palomino & Vergara, Misa, Bertola, Varela, Otaolaurruchi, Diestro, Lacave, Díaz Morales, Valderrama, Vergara & Gordon and later the very large firms of Williams & Humbert, Garvey, Diez-Mérito and Terry – this in addition to constructing new buildings for Bodegas Internacionales, the largest in Jerez.

In 1961, José María Ruíz-Mateos created a holding company RUMASA (abbreviated from Ruíz-Mateos Hermanos S.A.) to control his rapidly expanding empire, and in 1965 there was disagreement over the Harvey's contract and it was rescinded. But José María's ambitions ran far beyond controlling the sherry trade. During the '70s he took over many of the largest wine firms in the Rioja, Catalonia, Montilla, La Mancha and elsewhere, and soon the famous symbol of the industrious bee was going up on banks, property and construction companies, hotels, department stores, textile and chemical factories, and shipyards, while abroad RUMASA acquired the Augustus Barnett wine shops in England and another chain in Denmark. When the crash came in 1983 and the huge conglomerate was expropriated by the Spanish government, the Madrid daily *Diario 16* described Ruíz-Mateos as 'the man who wanted to buy Spain' and quipped that he had suggested to an astonished Spanish episcopacy (he is a devout Catholic) that one of his enterprises build for free any altar blessed by the Pope, on condition that the busy bee figured 'discreetly' on it.

The repercussions in Jerez were immediate and violent. There had been spectacular failures before, like that in 1879 of Julian Pemartín, who built himself a palace in the style of the Paris Opera House, but none that threatened the livelihood of half Jerez's inhabitants. The government stepped in at once to guarantee wages and appointed administrators to run the expropriated firms until such time as they could be sold to the private sector. This was to be a matter of years, because José María Ruíz-Mateos fought the expropriation tooth and nail, leaving the country at one point, only to be extradited and kept in custody for a spell; the case has still to be heard in the Spanish courts. To compound the difficulties, various firms, like the respected Cuvillo y Cia of Puerto de Santa María, geared to supplying RUMASA, were left with stocks on their hands which they could not sell and were bankrupted. The fact that RUMASA in its last days had dumped large stocks abroad caused prices to plummet, so adding to the difficulties of the remaining firms.

They have fought resolutely back, cooperating in a four-year plan to impose rigorous quality controls, fix minimum prices, cut stocks by allowing each firm a quota for exports and reducing the vineyard area from some 22,000 hectares to 19,000. These measures have gone a long way to restoring the situation. All the former RUMASA firms have now been returned to private ownership. Of the larger concerns, Bodegas Internacionales with its constituent companies (see page 140) and Diez-Mérito went to the financier Marcos Eguizábal, who took over Paternina and other RUMASA firms in the Rioja. Foreign investors have also shown their confidence in the future of sherry. Garvey, for example, being acquired by a West German supermarket group.

The most important development has, however, been the acquisition by Harvey's of Bristol – who, after breaking with RUMASA had already bought the bodegas of Mackenzie and Misa – of Terry and Palomino & Vergara, thus making this subsidiary of the British Allied Brewers the largest concern in Jerez. (The rival International Distillers & Vintners mounted its highly successful operation in Jerez some ten years ago by building the modern and extremely well-equipped Rancho Croft.) The sale of the last of the RUMASA bodegas, Williams & Humbert, has been delayed because José María Ruíz-Mateos maintained that the name 'Dry Sack' was his personal property. However, a court case in England has gone against him; and the firm has very recently been sold to Antonio Barbadillo, the well-known makers of *manzanilla* in Sanlúcar de Barrameda.

There was not so long ago a delightful and leisurely Britishness about Jerez, reminiscent of India in the days of the Raj and other outposts of Empire, with English the second, and sometimes the first, language in the bodegas (all the *bodegueros* and their families still speak it perfectly), a British Vice-Consul with his office at Williams & Humbert, and afternoon tea for wives and daughters (albeit at 8 p.m.) in the much lamented Hotel Los Cisnes. A lot of it, like the love for thoroughbred horses and polo – as much Jerezano as English – survives, but one senses a keener air blowing through the town as it braces itself for a more competitive future.

No community was ever closer knit by marriage than that of the aristocracy of the sherry trade. To quote from William Fifield's *The Sherry Royalty*:

> I suspect if you had to select one person as most intricately bound of all in this web you might choose Rafael Valdespino's wife, Margarita González Gilbey de Valdespino ... She had the Diez and Sandeman connections by her husband Rafael Valdespino, who is not only a Romate grandson by his paternal grandmother but a Guerrero grandson by his paternal grandmother. All these are big Sherry names. On her own, Margarita, by her father, the younger brother of Manuel González, is González and Gordon – first cousin of Mauricio González, of Beltrán Domecq, of José Ignacio Domecq &c. &c. Her delightful mother, Winifred Hilda Gilbey, still utterly English after half a century in Spain, was sister of Gordon Gilbey, head of Gilbey until his death in 1965. Another aunt of hers, a Gilbey sister too, is mother of Ian and Eric Mackenzie, directors of Mackenzie now a part of Harveys.

One regrets the disappearance of well-known names as the smaller bodegas are absorbed by the large international concerns. But even in the time of RUMASA, Bodegas Internacionales was being run by Don Beltrán Domecq, and scratch beneath the surface and you will find that these very concerns are being managed by the Ysasis, the Lacaves, the López de Carrizosas and others who once owned bodegas of their own. *Plus ça change, plus c'est la même chose.*

CHAPTER 3

Sherry and the Law

14 *The bodega of San Ginés, used by the Consejo Regulador for ceremonial functions*

The sherry region was one of the first in Europe to introduce regulations governing the production and sale of wine; in fact, the ordinances were so stringent as to go a long way towards crippling the trade. In October 1733, the Royal Council of Castile approved the establishment of the Gremio de la Vinatería (Guild of Vintners), whose far-reaching functions included the fixing of the price of grapes and of wine, both for home consumption and for export, the quota of butts to be despatched to Spanish America, the capacity of butts and maximum wages. The Guild also forbade the importation into the region of wines from other parts of Spain, except for export, and, with disastrous results, prohibited merchants from laying down sizeable stocks of wine. This extraordinary rule – which could have been drawn up only by an organisation headed by priests and bureaucrats and included just two wine-growers to represent the trade – caused long delays in preparing blends for shipment and was aimed at keeping profits in the hands of the growers and discouraging speculation in wine.

As Manuel M. González Gordon records, over the first forty years of the Guild's existence, its activities resulted in exports of sherry being limited to an annual average of only some 4,000 butts. By 1772, its members were already discussing whether the Guild should be dissolved; with foreign buyers turning to less trammelled regions, there were only nine shippers left in Jerez by 1754; and in 1834, amidst general relief, the Guild was dissolved.

It did one thing which is commemorated today – the adoption as its patron saint of San Ginés de la Jara (nothing, incidentally, to do with *jarras* or 'jugs', but the name of a rock rose growing in the neighbourhood where he lived) – to whom the annual harvest festival (see page 15) is dedicated and after whom the official bodega of the present controlling body, the Consejo Regulador, is named. On the walls of this beautiful arched building, which is used for ceremonial tastings, there is a series of quotations on sherry by famous writers, one for every year since 1971. It seems worth reproducing them:

1971 *Washington Irving*: God grant that I live long enough to drink all this wine and to be as happy as it can make me.

1972 *Pedro Antonio de Alarcón*: In each concentrated drop / is a thousand generations of destiny. / If worldly cares overwhelm you, / drink, o pilgrim, and you will swear that heaven is on earth.

1973 *Victor Hugo*: Long live sherry! Jerez is a city which should be in Paradise.

1974 *Somerset Maugham*: Sherry, the civilised drink.

1975 *Gregorio Marañón y Posadilla*: Sherry, masterwork of the Creation.

1976 *Manuel María González Gordon*: A meal without a glass of sherry beforehand is like a day that dawns without sun.

1977 *Lord Byron*: Here in Jerez I quaffed the famous wine at the fountain head.

1978 *Benito Perez Galdós*: If God had not made sherry, how imperfect his work would have been.

1979 *Alexander Fleming*: If penicillin cures illnesses, sherry revives the dead.

1980 *José María Pemán y Pemartín*: To drink in moderation / is to warm the heart / and without losing reason / give reason to life.

1981 *Pablo Neruda*: And the casks and cathedrals of sherry, / in whose Gongorine hearts / the topaz burns like a pale fire.

1982 A toast to *Franklin D. Roosevelt*: TO THE PRESIDENT OF THE UNITED STATES. (Proposed by Louis Howe on the night of 8 November 1932 on opening a bottle of sherry kept for twenty years in anticipation of the election of Roosevelt as President.)

1983 *William Shakespeare*: If I had a thousand sons, the first humane principle I would teach them should be, to forswear thin potations, and to addict themselves to sack.

1984 *Alexandre Dumas*: Sherry, symbol of joy and of the soul of Spain.

THE CONSEJO REGULADOR

It is often stated that the Consejo Regulador for Jerez–Xérès–Sherry, which dates from 1934, was the first of such bodies to be formed in Spain. To the best of my knowledge, this is not so, since it was predated by the Consejo Regulador for the Rioja in 1926.

Now known as the Consejo Regulador for Jerez–Xérès–Sherry and Manzanilla–Sanlúcar de Barrameda, it is headed by a President nominated by the Ministry of Agriculture and a Vice-President named by the Ministry of Commerce. It further numbers five members representing the growers, one from the co-operatives, one from the region as a whole and three from Jerez Superior, and five representing the bodegas and shippers. Two further members are appointed by the Ministry of Agriculture because of special knowledge of viticulture and oenology. An inspectorate attached to the administrative staff of the Consejo carries out regular checks in the vineyards and at the bodegas, working in collaboration with the Estación de Viticultura y Enología in Jerez.

Apart from keeping detailed records of the production and elaboration of the wines and authorising seals and labels to cover the amount, the work of the Consejo centres on the implementation of regulations with which a wine must conform to obtain *Denominación de Origen* (D.O.), corresponding to the French *Appellation d'Origine Contrôlée* (A.O.C.) or Italian *Denominazione di Origine Controllata* (D.O.C.) and formulated in accordance with the rules of the Office International du Vin (O.I.V.).

The regulations fall under two heads, those of the *Estatuto de la Viña*, *del Vino y de los Alcoholes*, a government decree promulgated in 1970 and applying to Spain as a whole, and the more detailed provisions of the *Reglamento de las Denominaciones de Origen 'Jerez–Xérès–Sherry' y 'Manzanilla–Sanlúcar de Barrameda'*, framed within the context of the *Estatuto*, but applying only to the sherry region.

The *Estatuto*, a lengthy document running to 134 *artículos* and some 20,000 words, embodies definitions of the different types of wines and alcoholic beverages; detailed rules for acceptable and unacceptable methods of viticulture, vinification and chemical composition; together with regulations covering records of production and the transport, distribution, sale and export of wines. It further bans the hybridisation of American and native wines and the irrigation of vineyards.

The provisions of the *Reglamento*, specific to the area, amount ultimately to restrictions designed to prevent the production of inferior wines. Again, the *Reglamento* is a voluminous document running to some 16,000 words, 59 *artículos* and scores of sub-sections, so that only some of the more important sections can be outlined here.

In the first place, it defines the demarcated area and lists the municipalities of the *zona de producción* as: Jerez de la Frontera, Puerto de Santa María, Sanlúcar de Barrameda and the areas within the municipal boundaries of Rota and Chipiona bordering Sanlúcar, which because of their *albariza* soils, situation and climate are suitable for the production of wines 'of superior quality'.

The permitted varieties of grape are described in Chapter 4 (under *Vine Varieties*). They are the Palomino de Jerez, Palomino Fino and Pedro Ximénez; the Moscatel is permissible only for wines labelled as such. In new plantations the different vine varieties may not be mixed.

The maximum density of plantation is 4,100 plants per hectare, and the maximum permitted yields are 80 hectolitres per hectare in Jerez Superior and 100 hectolitres in the rest of the demarcated area. Pruning must be by the traditional Jerezano method of *vara y pulgar*, leaving a maximum of eight buds on the fruit-bearing shoot. For the Pedro Ximénez and Moscatel, the Consejo authorises other systems. Only ripe and healthy fruit may be harvested, and sunning and 'plastering' must be carried out by traditional methods. (See Chapter 4 for details of these processes.)

Turning to vinification and elaboration, the yield must not be more than 72·5 litres of first run must from 100 kilograms of grapes. The must from subsequent pressings may not be used for wines with *denominación de origen*. The wines must be matured in bodegas situated within the towns of Jerez de la Frontera, Puerto de Santa María or Sanlúcar de Barrameda, or with special permission from the Consejo,

I
A selection of sherry labels

II
Sherry vineyards [overleaf]

III
*Pedro Domecq's
Macharnudo vineyards*

IV
*Vineyards in the
Macharnudo area*

in bodegas located within the vineyards of the demarcated area. *Manzanilla* must be matured in Sanlúcar de Barrameda. The wines must be matured in oak butts by the classical system of *criaderas* and *soleras* or as *añada* (vintage) wines. No wine less than three years old may be sold for consumption (see page 68). In the interests of quality, a minimum quantity of wine from Jerez Superior, fixed each year by the Consejo, must be used.

Article 15 defines the following styles of sherry: *fino*, *amontillado*, *oloroso*, *palo cortado*, *raya* and *manzanilla*. These are described in detail in Chapter 6. It also lays down specifications for *vino dulce* and *vino de color*, used in blending.

The Consejo Regulador maintains registers of:

1. Vineyards, with details of their location, extent and characteristics.

2. *Bodegas de Elaboración* (wine-making establishments, which mature the must for short periods before selling it).

3. *Bodegas de Producción* (wine-making establishments outside the *zona de crianza*, which sell must without maturing it).

4. *Bodegas de Crianza y Almacenado* (bodegas which mature and keep stocks of wine; these bodegas are required to have not less than 1,000 hectolitres of wine in the process of maturing, of which not less than 60 per cent must be from Jerez Superior).

5. *Bodegas de Crianza y Expedición* (bodegas in the *zonas de crianza* which mature and sell wines with *denominación de origen* for consumption; they must have in hand a minimum amount of 12,500 hectolitres of wine originating from registered vineyards and bodegas, of which 60 per cent must be from Jerez Superior; like the other classes of bodega which mature wine, they must of course possess sufficient oak butts to mature all the wine held in the bodega).

6. *Exportadores* (these are *Bodegas de Crianza y Expedición* holding a current licence from the Ministry of Commerce entitling them to export wine).

The *denominaciones de origen* 'Jerez–Xérès–Sherry' and 'Manzanilla–Sanlúcar de Barrameda' apply only to wines from registered vineyards and from *Bodegas de Crianza y Almacenado* and *Bodegas de Crianza y Expedición* inscribed in the Register. After the harvest the bodegas are required on 31 October of each year to submit records of the amount of must that they have obtained, differentiating between that from Jerez Superior and the rest of the zone. Prices for grapes and wine are fixed annually by the Consejo Regulador, and during the twelve months following 1 September of each year the bodegas may not ship more than 40 per cent of their stock of wine.

The Consejo is instructed to appoint a committee composed of three experts and a representative of the president to taste and report on the quality of all wines destined for both the home and foreign markets. All wines with *denominación de origen* must be sold in bottles with numbered seals and labelled with the insignia of the Consejo

15 *Control laboratory for ensuring that the rigorous standards of the Consejo Regulador are met*

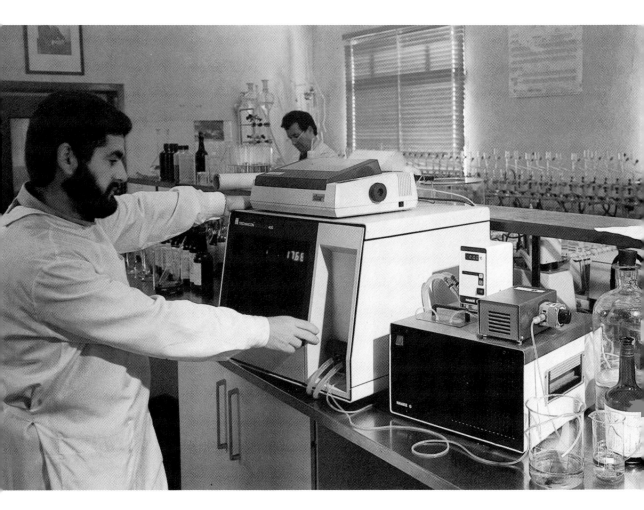

Regulador; if shipped in bulk, the containers must be of approved type and bear the seal of the Consejo Regulador. Wine shipped abroad must be accompanied with certificates of analysis and of *denominación de origen* in the form prescribed by INDO (Instituto Nacional de Denominaciones de Origen).

Apart from the government-controlled Consejo Regulador, the sherry industry has its own associations to represent it in matters of common interest such as labour, fiscal and trade affairs, relations with government departments, etc. Banded together as FEDEJEREZ to speak for the industry in dealings with the EEC, the individual associations are:

Asociación de Empresas Viñistas del Marco de Jerez (Vineyard Owners' Association, representing the owners of 30 per cent of the vineyards).

Asociación de Empresas de Elaboración y Crianza de Vino (Sherry Producers/Stockholders' Association, representing the holders of 95 per cent of sherry stocks).

Asociación de Criadores Exportadores de Sherry (Sherry Exporters Association – ACES, representing the companies responsible for 95 per cent of sherry sales worldwide).

Asociación de Empresas de Elaboración y Exportación de Bebidas (Brandy Producers' Association, representing the producers of 100 per cent of Brandy de Jerez sold worldwide, i.e. 95 per cent of all Spanish brandy).

A Consejo Regulador to administer a new *Denominación Específica 'Brandy de Jerez'* was set up only in 1987. Like the Consejo for 'Jerez–Xérès–Sherry' it is headed by a President appointed by the Ministry of Agriculture and includes similar government appointees, but numbers only seven members from the single body representing the producers, the Bodegas de Elaboración y Envejecimiento.

The *Reglamento* is much shorter and simpler than that for sherry. It sets out by stipulating that only brandies elaborated in Jerez de la Frontera, Puerto de Santa María and Sanlúcar de Barrameda qualify for *denominación de origen* and that they must be made by traditional methods. Jerez brandy must be made from *aguardiente de vino* (grape spirit), of which the different types are defined, and the use of neutral spirit from other sources is totally forbidden. Maturation must be carried out either in *criaderas* and *soleras* as in making sherry, or by static maturation in a single oak barrel as in making an *añada* or vintage sherry.

Three different classes of Jerez brandy are defined as: *Solera, Solera Reserva* and *Solera Gran Reserva*. Each must be aged for a minimum period and contain not less than a specified amount of the 'non-alcohols' which give a brandy its flavour (for details, see page 98).

As in the case of sherry, the Consejo is instructed to set up an expert *Comité de Calificación* to keep watch on the quality of Jerez brandies.

The only Register is that of the *Bodegas de Elaboración y Envejecimiento* and any establishment making Jerez brandy qualifying for *denominación de origen* must also be registered for the making and maturing of sherry in accordance with the rules of the *Reglamento* for 'Jerez–Xérès–Sherry'.

BRITISH AND FOREIGN SHERRIES

The labelling of sherry-type wines made abroad is a very sore issue in Jerez de la Frontera and has frequently been the subject of litigation. The *bodegueros* feel particularly strongly about British sherry, which has been making inroads into their major market in the United Kingdom, unfairly as they consider, since through some official quirk it is taxed at a lower rate than the genuine article! Comparative figures for United Kingdom sales over the last decade were:

UK sales of sherry and sherry-style wines (*per cent*)

	1979	1986	1987
Sherry	47	43	41
British sherry	37	43	45
Cyprus sherry	12	7	6
Other	2	1	1
Montilla	2	6	7

The difficulty in taking legal action against the use of the word 'sherry' for British-made wine is that its manufacture has a very long history and the term is well-established by usage.

As long ago as 1635, one Francis Chamberlayne was granted exclusive rights to make and sell wine produced from 'dried grapes or raysons'. By the middle of the nineteenth century some 600,000 gallons were being produced from these and other fruits and being sold or fraudulently blended with imported wines. With the introduction at the turn of the century of methods of concentrating grape juice into a syrup easily transportable in drums, the industry gathered impetus, and by 1965 more than 9 million gallons of such British wine (not all of it, of course, 'sherry') was being made and sold.

The Sherry Shippers' Association, a London-based consortium of the leading shippers, fired the first shot in their campaign to protect the name in 1925, when it brought an action under the Merchandise Marks Act of 1887 against a concern selling British-made 'Corona Pale Sherry'. However, the Association stopped short of prosecuting firms using the description 'British sherry', nor did it proceed against the vendors of 'Cyprus sherry', 'Australian sherry' or 'South African sherry'.

It was, ironically enough, the action of the small Spanish Costa Brava Wine Company in selling a 'Spanish champagne' in England which brought matters to a head. After three years of legal battles, the champagne producers in 1960 obtained a High Court ruling that the word 'champagne' might be used only for wine produced in the Champagne district of France.

The implications were at once obvious. If it was illegal to label Perelada 'Spanish champagne', what justification could there be for 'British sherry'? It was, however, the makers of British wines, notably Vine Products Ltd of Kingston-upon-Thames, who, apprehensive as to the implications of the 'Spanish champagne' case, struck first by seeking a decision in the High Court that the description 'British sherry' did not infringe the rights of the Spanish shippers.

The case opened in the Chancery Division of the High Court before Mr Justice Cross on 9 February 1967 and lasted for twenty-nine days, the shippers calling in, among others, the President of the Consejo Regulador and a Professor of Arabic Studies from Madrid University to give evidence on their behalf. Counsel for Vine Products argued that the name 'British sherry' was sanctioned by long usage, producing thousands of wine lists and scores of labels to prove that this was so.

On 31 July 1967, Mr Justice Cross delivered judgement, ruling that the word 'sherry' by itself means wine produced in the Jerez district of

Spain, but that the Spanish producers had acquiesced for so long with the descriptions such as 'British sherry', 'Cyprus sherry', 'Australian sherry' and the rest that it was too late to object to such descriptions.

Although the judgement put a stop to some major abuses, such as the advertisement of British sherry by pictures of girls in flamenco costume or the claim of the South Africans that a reason for drinking their sherry-type wine was *because it is real sherry*, it left the shippers unhappy. The issue was raised officially when Spain joined the Common Market, but it seems that there was some hard bargaining over fishing rights in British waters, and the Jerezanos were fobbed off with a promise that the issue would be raised again in 1995. With the tide running strongly against such descriptions as 'Australian Burgundy' or 'Spanish Chablis', which have virtually been discontinued, and with geographical descriptions being reserved for wines from the region in question, it is to be hoped that it is only a matter of time before the Jerezanos obtain their rights.

There does not, however, appear to be much rhyme or reason about the law in such matters. In 1979 a group of sherry shippers sought an injunction in the British courts to prevent the use in Britain of the terms *fino, amontillado* and *oloroso* to describe the different styles of the sherry-like wines from the neighbouring Spanish region of Montilla–Moriles. After the case had dragged on for six years agreement was reached in the High Court that the names should no longer be used. This disregards the fact that the wines are legitimately described as *fino, amontillado* and *oloroso* in Spain itself, and that in the first place the Jerezanos actually borrowed the word *amontillado* from Montilla!

As to the quality of overseas 'sherry', I recently came across an interview in the Spanish gastronomic magazine *Club de Gourmets* with the illustrious Professor Olmo, now in his fifty-fifth year at Davis University in California. Asked what he thought about the use of the word 'sherry' for other sherry-style wines, he replied: 'In the United States there has been little effective publicity for Jerez. At present there is a tendency to drink Californian or New York State sherry.' At this his interviewer, Paz Ivison (a good Jerezano name), interjected that she had tried a 'sherry neoyorkino' and had nearly died of shock. The Professor smiled and said: 'Yes – that's why we are drinking more and more proper "Tío Pepe" in California.'

I myself have come to grips with this. Some Christmases ago I received a call from the BBC saying that as part of their festivities they wished to transmit a 'blind' tasting of sherries live to test whether an 'expert' could in fact distinguish between sherry from Spain and British sherry. I pointed out that there were people a great deal more expert than I, but it transpired that no-one from the trade or official organisations was willing to cooperate.

Cursing myself for being talked into it, I found myself on a train for Bristol a day or two later. It is a somewhat unnerving experience to be invited to make a sally of oneself in front of an audience of a few million. I succeeded in identifying a 'Don Zoilo' *fino* and Harvey's 'Bristol Cream' by name (but I would agree with what Professor Peynaud says on the subject of identifying wines by name at blind tastings – it is more luck than good management) and identified two other sherries as from Spain, but came to grief over one from South Africa, having been informed by the BBC that they were all either from Spain or Britain. However, I *did* pick out the three British sherries without hesitation – it was the first time I had ever encountered one, and whatever their other virtues they did not to me taste of sherry at all. As to how they had been made, I remain in ignorance to this day, since the BBC camera unit that went to photograph at Kingston-upon-Thames was turned away at the gate of the plant.

Perhaps the oddest twist in the story of British sherry is that both Vine Products Ltd, which is making such inroads into the market for sherry, and Harveys of Bristol, now the biggest grouping in Jerez with its acquisition of Terry and Palomino & Vergara, belong to the self-same Allied Brewers, which also has a large stake in Pedro Domecq.

CHAPTER 4

Soils, Vines and Vineyards

The demarcated region, roughly triangular in shape, is situated between the River Guadelete to the east, the Atlantic to the south and the Guadalquivir to the west and north. The land lies within the municipal limits of Puerto Real and Chiclana de la Frontera in the south; of Jerez de la Frontera in the centre; of Puerto de Santa María, Rota, Chipiana and Sanlúcar de Barrameda, westwards along the Atlantic coast; and of Trebujena and Lebrija to the north. Within the region is an area known as Jerez Superior, which because of its *albariza* soils, geographical situation and microclimate, makes the best wines.

The extent of land under vines belonging to the different townships is shown in the table overleaf.

According to the figures of the Consejo Regulador, there are 6,945 individual vineyards belonging to 5,200 proprietors. A few of the largest sherry firms own as much as 2,000 hectares, but most of the vineyards are small, 4,897 of them being of less than 12·5 hectares.

16 Palomino grapes in the vineyards of Croft

Area of sherry vineyards (hectares) in 1985

Municipality	Jerez Superior	Other	Total
Jerez de la Frontera	10,192·88	445·45	10,693·33
Puerto de Sta María	1,219·60	141·33	1,360·93
Sanlúcar de Barrameda	1,634·90	519·38	2,154·28
Chiclana de la Frontera		2,021·86	2,021·86
Puerto Real		1,051·26	1,051·26
Rota	171·75	327·44	499·20
Chipiona	65·17	708·74	773·91
Trebujena		867·39	857·39
Lebrija		211·72	211·72
Total	13,284·31	6,295·57	19,579·88

Most of the growers own their land and some 30 per cent of them sell their fruit to one or other of the seven co-operatives in the region to be vinified. The co-operative may then, like CAYDSA, mature the wine in its own *soleras*, but more often sells it to one of the *bodegas de crianza* (see page 41) for elaboration.

SOILS AND CLIMATE

The best of the soils for viticulture are the *albarizas* dating from the Tertiary era and formed by the sedimentation of marine diatoms in the seawater of the period. They are therefore rich in calcium carbonate, containing between 30 and 40 per cent, and are typically composed of some 50 to 60 per cent of clay, 30 to 40 per cent of mud and 15 to 20 per cent of sand. The *albariza* vineyards march across a series of low, gently sloping hills, dark green in summer and a sparkling white in the winter sunshine when the vegetation dies down. The soils readily absorb air and water, expanding above the level of the access roads, which are often planted with retaining hedges of prickly pear. One of their great virtues is that they dry without cracking, sealing in and slowly releasing moisture to the deep-rooted vines during the long rainless summers. The yield is comparatively low, amounting on average to about eight to nine butts (of 500 to 550 litres) per *aranzada* of 0·475 hectares or 1·174 acres, but the quality of the wine high.

Probably the best of the *albariza* districts, yielding the most delicate musts, are those of Balbaina and Añina, close to the sea and producing the best *finos*, followed by Macharnudo and further inland, Carrascal, which gives rise to fuller-bodied wines. Other very highly rated districts are those of Carrahola, San Julián, Los Tercios, Corchuelo and Montana.

The other types of soil give larger yields of wine, but of coarser quality. *Barro* contains less limestone, normally about 30 per cent, with clay and sand in varying proportions and decomposed organic matter, and is darker in colour because of the presence of iron oxide. It is found in the valley bottoms and, interspersed with sand, along the coast almost the whole way from Sanlúcar to Gibraltar, and yields about 20 per cent more must per hectare than *albariza*, usually more fully-bodied and not as clean. Its higher fertility results in the prolific growth of weeds, so that it requires more tilling than the other soils.

Arena contains over 70 per cent of sand, together with clay and no more than 19 per cent of limestone; it is easily tilled and yields are prolific – some 50 per cent above those from *albariza* – but the quality of the wine is poor.

Very few of the vineyard areas, or *pagos* as they are known in the sherry district, are completely uniform in soil type, and the colour of the foliage and quality of the must may vary from one part to another of a large vineyard. The growers distinguish between different categories of *albariza*, among them: *tajón*, hard, compact and containing some 80 per cent of calcium carbonate; *lantejuela*, a friable variant with about 50 per cent calcium carbonate; and *barrajuela*, a much esteemed chalky soil, again with some 50 per cent of calcium carbonate, streaked with ochre. Outside the *albariza* area, the rich and fertile soils of Chipiona to the far south of the region produce large amounts of an inexpensive *fino* type wine, pleasant enough for quaffing with food.

Jerez enjoys a generally balmy climate, the breezes from the nearby Bay of Cádiz moderating the summer heat. The climate rather echoes the difference between the British and Spanish characters; it is rarely overcast and cloudy, but either unbrokenly sunny or, on rare occasions, pelting with rain. In hard figures, the average maximum temperatures vary from 16°C in winter to 31°C in summer and the average minima from 5·4°C in winter to 16°C in summer. The average annual rainfall is 650 millimetres or 25·6 inches, though in exceptional years twice or half as much has been recorded. Almost all of it falls during the winter and early spring and there is virtually no rain from

June to October. The average number of wet days is 75 in a year, and in 1945 there were only 53.

The predominating winds are from the south and south-west, off the Atlantic, and benefit the vines by depositing dew during the dry season. There is also the occasional *levante*, a dry, hot wind from the east, which can penetrate any but the closest fitting window, depositing a fine sand. In general, the climate varies so little from year to year that, quite apart from the *solera* system which ensures uniform quality, there is usually no great difference in the wines from one vintage to another.

VINE VARIETIES

In the past, large numbers of different vine varieties were grown in the sherry region; the number was much reduced during the nineteenth century and now only three are authorised for new plantations: the Palomino, Pedro Ximénes and Moscatel. Of these, the Palomino is much the most important.

It is cultivated up and down Spain, sometimes under the name of the 'Jerez' – in the Duero valley, Galicia, Extremadura, Aragón and Catalonia – but is native to Andalucía and some 68·5 per cent is grown in the province of Cádiz. In his *Diccionario del vino de Jerez*, Julián Pemartín, suggests that it was named after Don Fernán Núñez Palomino, one of the knights who fought for King Alfonso X during the reconquest of Jerez from the Moors. Be this as it may, the grape is also known as the Listán; as the Palomina, Palomilla and Palomillo in other parts of Andalucía and in the Canaries; as the Colombard in France; as the Horgazuela in Puerto de Santa María; as the Tempranilla (not to be confused with the black Tempranillo of the Rioja) in Rota and Trebujena; and as the Ojo de Liebre (not to be confused with the black Ull de Llebre of Catalonia) in Lebrija.

There are, in fact, two Palominos. The Palomino de Jerez or Palomino Basto, with which the region was planted in the past, has largely been replaced with the Palomino Fino, a sub-variety from Sanlúcar de Barrameda, which has proved better both in terms of yield and the quality of the wine. It produces large bunches of grapes, medium-sized and golden in colour when they ripen in early September. The must is colourless and sweet. It makes refreshing but somewhat neutral beverage wines lacking in acidity, but comes into its own when matured under *flor* by the *solera* system, giving rise to a whole gamut of sherries, intense and aromatic.

In recent years much work has been carried out, both at the Instituto Nacional de Investigaciones Agrarias and in the nurseries of the large firms, such as González Byass, into developing improved strains of Palomino. In the first place, individual plants are selected, the criteria being that they are healthy, resistant to disease and produce good (but not excessive) yields of high quality must. The chosen plants are then sent to Davis University in California or to Madrid for heat treatment and are returned free of virus. They are cloned (i.e. vegetatively reproduced by division of the plants), then grafted on to virus-resistant stocks, also subjected to heat treatment, and planted in sterilised soil. The trials have been highly successful in evolving plants resistant to pests, such as nematodes, prevalent in the *albariza* soil.

Next of importance in the sherry region, the Pedro Ximénez has been cultivated in Spain, mainly in Andalucía, since very early times. Its legendary origins have been described by every writer on sherry from the famous Simon de Roxas Clemente downwards. Julian Jeffs, who investigated it in detail, reluctantly discounts the story, but who am I to omit it? The vine, it is said, originated in the Canary Islands and was taken via Madeira to the Rhine. From there, at the time of the Emperor Charles V's campaigns in the Low Countries in the sixteenth century, one of his soldiers, a certain Peter Siemens (or, in Spanish, Pedro Simón) brought it to Málaga. In support of this, it is suggested that the grape is identical with the German Elbling.

In the sherry region it is grown on the lower slopes of the *albariza* vineyards and harvested in early September, when it produces intensely sweet grapes, whose sugar content is still further increased by sunning, and is used for sweet dessert wines. In neighbouring Montilla–Moriles, where it is the principal vine variety, it is picked while waxy white and if fermented at once and to completion, it produces bone-dry *montillas*. In the sherry region it is more difficult to grow and more prone to disease than the Palomino, and plantings are on the decrease, especially as it has been found possible to make very satisfactory sweetening wines from sun-dried Palomino. Much of the Pedro Ximénez (or PX) wine for cream sherries and sweet *olorosos* has traditionally been imported from Montilla–Moriles and it seems that threatened EEC regulations forbidding the movement of wine from one demarcated region to another may possibly pose a serious threat to the huge PX *soleras* destined for sherries such as 'Bristol Cream'.

The Moscatel or Muscat grape takes its name from the Latin *musca* (or 'fly'), because flies are so partial to its sweet and fragrant grapes. It has been grown in the Mediterranean area from the very earliest times and was described by Pliny; it was certainly cultivated in Andalucía, especially around Málaga, in Roman times. It is still grown there and also in large amount in the Valencian area, both for wine-making and dessert grapes, and in limited amounts in the sherry region for making sweet wines (if not for adding to *fino* as suggested at a recent *Decanter* tasting panel!). The Moscatel wines are made in similar fashion to the Pedro Ximénez by sun-drying the grapes, though for a rather shorter period. This so increases the sugar content that much of it is left after fermentation finishes. The Moscatel grapes grown in the *arena* soils of Chipiona are larger but less delicate and fruity than the smaller Jerez variety.

CULTIVATION

Ever since the invasion of the vineyards by phylloxera in 1894–8, the native vines, as in most other parts of the world, have been grafted on to American root stocks resistant to the destructive aphid, ever present in the soil except in some of the sandier *arena* areas. The stocks are chosen from those most suited to soils with high lime content, and among those most used are the Chasselas x Berlandieri 41 B (Millardet) and the Chasselas x Berlandieri 333 M (Montpellier). For soils containing less lime the Riparia x Berlandieri 161–49 (Couderc) is a favourite. Grafting may be carried out in the vineyard, but bench grafting in which the cuttings are grafted in the nursery, is becoming increasingly common.

In the past the vines were most often planted in a diamond-shaped pattern known as *trebosillo*. With the need to economise on labour and to use tractors for tilling, the alternative square-shaped system of *marco real* is now in general use. The vines were formerly planted at the corners of a square either 1·56 x 1·56 or 1·50 x 1·50 metres, but to allow for the passage of tractors, a width of 2·30 to 2·40 metres is now allowed for the lanes between the rows of vines, while in the other direction the distance between rows is 1·15 to 1·20 metres. The *Reglamento* (page 40) permits a maximum density of plantation of 4,100 vines per hectare.

In most Spanish vineyards the vines are grown low without support from wires or stakes. In the sherry region it was formerly the practice to prop the branches individually with *tutores* (stakes) or *horquillas* (forked sticks), but in the wake of mechanisation, these have now been scrapped in favour of *espalderas*, in which the vines are supported by wires strung from one end of the row of vines to the other. Expensive to install, the system nevertheless cuts down labour and in the long run reduces costs.

The low-growing vines of other regions are pruned by the method of *poda en vaso* ('goblet-shaped'), and in the Penedès the French Guyot method has been introduced for acclimatised vines; in Jerez an entirely distinct and traditional method of *poda de vara y pulgar* is employed. In the case of the Palomino the *vara*, or branch which is to bear the current crop, is left with seven or eight buds, and the *pulgar* (literally 'thumb'), a short shoot which will become next year's *vara*, with only one. The technique of pruning is devised to foster the healthy growth of the plant and to prolong its life. For example, all the cuts are made on the same side of the branch, the so-called *carrera de secos*, so leaving the other side, the *carrera de verdes*, unobstructed for the free flow of sap.

The other vine varieties are usually pruned by the same method, but other methods of pruning are also permitted. Apart from the all-important *poda*, carried out in December or January, unwanted shoots are pruned in the spring so as to remove all but the wanted buds and to concentrate the energies of the plant. This operation is known as *castra*, or *recastra*, if performed a second time.

Work in the vineyards proceeds the year round. After the last of the harvest, the vines are examined so that any that are defective may later be replaced. Most of the vineyards are on gentle hill slopes, and to prevent the autumn rains draining downhill and eroding the soil, it was formerly the custom to box in the vines individually by digging a pit around each plant and heaping the sides with earth, an operation known as *alumbra*. This channelled the rain where it was most needed around the roots, but in these days of spiralling labour costs pits are no longer dug around the vines, but mechanically in the alleys between them.

At the time of the pruning in late December or January, the pits (or *piletas*) are levelled out and the soil is tilled deeply either once or twice before the vines bud in March. Lighter tilling is carried out at intervals during the growing season, both to remove weeds and to smooth the surface of the soil and cover cracks through which underground moisture might evaporate.

The most serious diseases of the vine to affect the sherry region are mildew (*Plasmopara viticola*) and oidium (*Uncinula necator*). Given the dry climate, neither poses a serious threat, and when outbreaks occur it is usually in wet years during May or June. Oidium is controlled by dusting the vines with sulphur and mildew by spraying them with 'Bordeaux mixture' or the more modern Cuprosan. In the large vineyards this is done with helicopters. There is also a variety of insect pests. These are nowadays countered by sophisticated chemicals, but, as Manuel M. González Gordon relates in his *Sherry, The Noble Wine*, growers had their own effective ways of dealing with them in the past:

> Hidalgo in his *Efemérides*, referring to the seventeenth century, mentions an insect called the *purgón*, which must be presumed to be the *pulgón de las viñas* (*Altica oleracea*, or vine grub), and writes: '. . . at the municipal meeting fo 10 April 1600 (page 1609) Don Diego Caballero de los Olivos (24th Alderman) proposes that 'the *purgón* be excommunicated [*sic*] as it has produced such havoc in the vineyards' and it was decided to offer special prayers in Jerez. . .
>
> In 1640 there was another plague of *pulgón* in Jerez; more prayers were said, and it was attributed to this act of piety that the blight disappeared.

HARVESTING

Las niñas y la viñas difíciles son de guardar (Girls and vineyards are difficult to guard). So the old Jerezano proverb – and it is as the vintage approaches that the grapes are at their most tempting. It was, in fact, at one time customary to erect small huts on stilts (in Spanish, *bienteveo*, 'I see you well') manned by an armed guard to deter intruders. Because it is so far south, the traditional date for the beginning of the vintage in Jerez is 8 September, the Feast of the Nativity of Our Lady, rather than late September or even October in more northerly regions of Spain. Nowadays the exact date is set very precisely by laboratory measurements of the sugar and acid content of the grapes, which lie between 11° and 13° Baumé and 2·5 to 3·5 grams of acid (expressed as tartaric) per litre of must. Different grape varieties are picked separately, though 85 per cent of the vineyards are now planted with Palomino.

The harvest (or *vendimia*) lasts for about a month; the leaves are still green when it starts, but turning to russet or gold by the time the last of the fruit is garnered. The pickers, mostly men, wearing colourful cotton shirts and straw hats or stripped to the waist, cut the bunches of grapes with a knife and put them into plastic boxes holding some 10 to 12 kilograms of grapes, differently coloured for the large bodegas – red for González Byass, blue for Domecq and yellow and black for others. The containers are straightway loaded into trucks and taken to the vinification plant, where the grapes arrive within a quarter of an hour of being picked, so avoiding bruising of the fruit with the consequent spillage of must and premature fermentation or the discoloration of the must by pigments from the skins.

V
Palomino grapes, the predominant sherry variety

VI
A vineyard house

VII
*Harvest in the vineyards
of Pedro Domecq*

VIII
*The old method
of 'sunning' grapes on
esparto mats (see the
illustration on page 57
for the modern method)*

IX
*Growing virus-free
Palomino clones in the
nurseries of González
Byass*

X
*Treading the grapes in
traditional fashion*

In the past, when it was customary for all the grapes to be sunned before fermentation, the procedure was rather different. They were picked into baskets made of olive shoots or into large wooden panniers slung over the shoulder by a strap and carried to a building in the vineyard, housing the *lagares* where the grapes were trodden, and laid on esparto grass mats in the open air, where they were left to dry for at least twelve to twenty-four hours. Nowadays, only a very small proportion of grapes – those destined for the fuller-bodied *olorosos* or sweet wines, such as PX – are sunned, and the procedure is different. The bunches are laid in long lines on esparto grass mats and protected from the dew at night by plastic covers supported on hoops, thus reducing the number of days that they need be exposed to the sun. Apart from concentrating the must and increasing the sugar content of the grapes, sunning has other effects, such as raising the total acidity and nitrogen content, but at the same time destroying malic acid, so altering the nose and flavour of the wine. With *finos*, which now constitute the bulk of sherries, the object is to obtain the freshest possible wine, hence the emphasis on transporting the fruit to the bodega with the minimum of delay.

17 *Sunning of grapes in the vineyards of González Byass to make sweet wine*

CHAPTER 5

Making and Maturing Sherry

VINIFICATION

Every visitor to a sherry bodega is shown the traditional cowhide *zapatos de pisar*, the nail-studded boots used for treading the grapes during most of the long centuries of making sherry. It is only during the last few decades that treading has been abandoned in favour of mechanical presses.

It was a picturesque operation. The bunches of grapes were tipped into square wooden troughs known as *lagares* and housed in the low white buildings which crown each vineyard. There were four men,

18 *Working the scales at Wisdom & Warter*

bare-legged and in shorts and cotton shirts, to each *lagar*, and they began work at about midnight, continuing until midday and resting during the heat of the day. This also had the advantage that fermentation was delayed during the cool of the night. Unlike their counterparts in the port region, 'crazy Bacchants' as Rupert Croft-Cooke described them, moving in time to a band, the *pisadores* in Jerez marched calmly and steadily from one side of the *lagar* to the other. It is important that the stems and pips, which impart bitter elements to the must, should not be crushed, and it was found that the weight of a man exerts just the right pressure on the grapes. Again, the tacks in the boots soon picked up grape skins, so presenting a smooth surface and avoiding rupture. The free-running must was collected in barrels, and the remaining pulp was packed around a tall metal screw, held in place by an esparto grass mat, and pressed between wooden blocks.

As regards the quality of must, this was probably the ideal way of crushing and pressing grapes, but labour-intensive as it is, it was inevitable that it should give way to mechanical pressing. Once the problem of contamination by iron, which causes turbidity in the wine, had been overcome by the use of stainless steel, such presses proved very successful.

Modern practice is for the grapes to be lightly crushed between rubber rollers. A small amount of *yeso* or gypsum (0·75 to 1 gram per kilogram of grapes) is added in the interests of obtaining brighter, slightly more acid must, and the slurry is then pumped to the presses.

These may be of three types. The first is the horizontal hoop and chain pattern in which the pulp is gradually compressed between metal plates, the must running out through the slatted wooden sides. Another form of batch press is the Willmes, of German design, in which an inflatable rubber bag presses the pulp against the inside of a stainless steel cylinder, thus avoiding any possibility of rupturing residual pips or stalks. The cylinder may then be rotated, so redistributing the load, and the process repeated as often as desired.

The most modern presses, such as those first used by Harveys and Barbadillo at their modern Gibalbín winery and by Croft, are continuous and completely different in design. The grapes are fed by an Archimedean screw up a long inclined stainless steel cylinder with a perforated base. Much of the juice or must separates and drains away at once and is used for making *fino*. At the end of the cylinder is a moveable shutter and by opening or closing this to the required degree, varying pressure can be exerted on the contents. Musts obtained with intermediate pressures are used for *oloroso* and the rest for distillation. The *Reglamento* (see page 40) lays down that not more

19 *Modern continuous press at the Croft bodegas*

20 *Archimedean screw in a modern continuous press, producing must of different qualities by varying the pressure*

than 72·5 litres of virgin must, or 70 litres once separated from the
lees, may be extracted from 100 kilograms of grapes. Must obtained at
a higher rate of extraction may not be used for wines with
denominación de origen.

The must was traditionally fermented in oak butts of 500 to 600
litres filled to 80 per cent of their capacity. This method was used until
quite recently at Sandeman's, and still is at a highly conservative
bodega such as Valdespino. There is much to be said for it, since the
ratio of surface area to volume for a small cask is high, and in a hot
climate, such as that of Jerez, the heat of fermentation is quicky
radiated. Although the butts were subsequently often sold to the
distilleries in Scotland for maturing their whisky, it was obvious that in
an age of high technology, it was too expensive both in terms of the
expensive oak barrels and of labour. An alternative method is to
ferment in earthenware *tinajas*. I had thought that these were used
only in Montilla–Moriles, but have been surprised to see them in large
numbers at Sandeman, Garvey and CAYDSA in Sanlúcar de
Barrameda. However, the method of the future is in large tanks,
preferably temperature-controlled. The must is first left in large
depósitos for solid matter to settle out before being pumped into them.

The best but most expensive material is stainless steel, and the tanks
are usually of 8,000 to 25,000 litres capacity, but may be as large as
300,000. The temperature of the fermenting must, which rises quicky
and spontaneously, is controlled either by running water down the
sides of the tank or with a heat exchanger. It is ideally kept to between
20°C and 26°C and should never rise above 30°C. An alternative and
less expensive form of tank is made of polyester resin reinforced with
fibreglass; in these the temperature is lowered by adding fresh must
and kept to between 29°C and 30°C. A third and ingenious form of
tank I have seen only at Osborne's Atalaya winery in Puerto de Santa
María. Made of epoxy-lined steel, this is horizontal rather than vertical
and is not fully filled, so that fermentation approximates more to the
traditional method in oak butts. This method gives excellent results but
is too expensive to be adopted generally.

Depending upon the temperature, the first or tumultuous
fermentation, so-called because the liquid literally seems to boil, lasts
for three days to a week. It is brought about by yeasts which occur
naturally on the skins of the grapes and give them their 'bloom'; it is
not customary to use cultivated yeasts in Jerez, though Pedro Domecq
make use of a pure strain, which they have themselves isolated, first
disinfecting the must with a little sulphur dioxide.

At the end of tumultuous fermentation almost all of the grape sugar

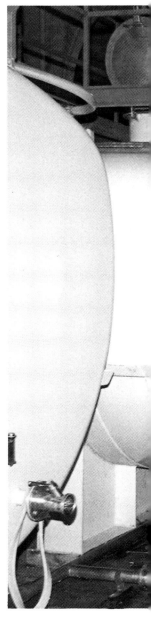

21 *Steel fermentation tanks of novel horizontal design at the Osborne bodegas near Puerto de Santa María* has been transformed into alcohol and carbon dioxide. A much slower secondary fermentation then sets in, during which a whole diversity of organic compounds, glycerine, acids, aldehydes, esters and the rest, most in small amount, is evolved. At the end of December or in January, the turbid must (as it is called in Jerez until it passes to the

criadera) 'falls bright' as suspended matter falls to the bottom of the tanks. At this point the must is traditionally classified, butt by butt, or tank by tank, for colour, clarity, aroma and palate. This is done by the *capataz* (or head cellarman) so as to separate the wines suitable for biological ageing under *flor* as *finos* from the others, which will undergo a physico-chemical ageing process. The *capataz* marks the containers with a series of conventional signs, indicating the type of sherry for which he considers the contents most suited:

/	*raya = fino*
/*	*una raya un punto* = to be decided
//	*dos rayas = oloroso*
///	*tres rayas = raya*
##	*Parrilla* = no good

The must is now racked (or decanted) off the lees, a sludge consisting of any remaining solid matter such as skins, pips, dead yeasts, etc, and is for the first time described as 'wine'. At this point the wine earmarked for *fino*, which will grow a *flor* (see below), is lightly fortified with *mitad y mitad*, a fifty-fifty mixture of grape alcohol and sherry, to between 15° and 16° (percentage by volume of alcohol), while that for *olorosos* and *rayas* is brought up to 18° with straight grape spirit to prevent the growth of *flor*. At this stage the wine is checked again by the *capataz*, and if he cannot make up his mind as to how it will develop it is removed to the traditional butts, where it remains for periods of up to a year awaiting further classification and is known as *mosto sobretablas*. The rest of the wine, classified according to type, is transferred to the butts of the appropriate *criadera* or 'nursery', in which it will mature.

In fact, the sampling and laboratory analysis of must prior to harvesting and modern techniques of pressing have taken a great deal of guesswork out of sherry-making; *all* of the free-run must from the new continuous presses is used for making *fino* without the need for further classification.

THE SHERRY FLOR

The *flor* (literally 'flower') which grows spontaneously on the surface of certain wines and to which the *finos* owe their distinctive nose and flavour is unique to Jerez (and one or two other regions of Spain, such as Montilla and Rueda, producing wines of the same general type).

XI
Carboys of cultivated
flor *at the bodegas of*
Duff Gordon

XII
*Branding a new butt at
Pedro Domecq*

XIII
*Charring the inside of a
new butt in the coopery
at Sandeman's*

Although samples of *flor* have been taken from Jerez and used to inoculate 'sherry' type wines produced elsewhere, it never appears of its own accord.

The *flor* is, in fact, a yeast, or mixture of yeasts of the genus *Saccharomyces*, derived from those present in the last stages of fermentation, principally *S. ellipsoideus*, *S. mangini* and *S. oviformis*. Under the new conditions of increased alcoholic degree, the yeasts rise spontaneously to the surface of the wine, and their metabolism changes from the production of alcohol in anaerobic conditions (i.e. in the absence of air) to an aerobic metabolism entirely different in character. In the new aerobic stage four varieties of *Saccharomyces* are responsible for the biological ageing of sherry: *S. cheriensis*, *S. beticus*, *S. montuliensis* and *S. rouxii*.

Among the conditions under which *flor* will form are that the grape sugar must be fermented out, that the surface of the wine must be exposed to air and may not be disturbed, that the temperature is as uniform as possible and between 15° and 20°C, and that the alcoholic strength is preferably between 15° and 15·5° (per cent by volume). In practice, the wine is kept in 500-litre butts, five-sixths filled and only loosely stoppered with a wooden bung; once it appears, the *flor* grows rapidly to form a wrinkled layer (*velo*) on the interface of the wine. In the dry atmosphere of Jerez de la Frontera, it is thickest and lightest in colour during the spring and autumn, thinning out in summer and winter, when the dead cells sink to the bottom of the barrel. In the seaside towns of Sanlúcar de Barrameda and Puerto de Santa María, where temperatures are more even and the atmosphere more humid, it remains thick and pure white in colour all year round, and it is in these places that the best *finos* are made.

Flor grows best in old butts, and I was once shown a *solera* in Sanlúcar where it was thick and pure white, but the replacement of only a single stave with new wood in one of the casks had resulted in a much thinner, yellow-coloured growth. If, on the other hand, wine is kept in the same butt and not 'refreshed', it will normally breed *flor* for some six to eight years, after which it dies and sinks to the bottom of the butt, the *fino* then developing into an *amontillado* (see page 61). In a *solera*, where there is continuous replenishment of old wine by new, the *flor* renews itself indefinitely.

Recent work carried out by Soledad Sollero at Pedro Domecq underlines the complex effects of biological ageing under *flor*. In the first place the layer of yeasts protects the wine from oxidation and destroys any traces of *Mycoderma aceti*, which would otherwise in the presence of air turn the wine into vinegar.

The other effects of biological ageing can be summarised as follows:

1 Volatile acidity is markedly reduced, with loss of acetic acid and also of ethyl acetate. Of the fixed (involatile) acids, malic acid is in the first place converted to lactic through the malo-lactic fermentation; thereafter there is a reduction in the amounts of all the fixed acids: tartaric, pyruvic, malic and lactic. When biological ageing eventually terminates with the death of the *flor* and the *fino* begins turning into *amontillado*, there is a general increase in acidity and deepening of colour due to oxidation.

2 During biological ageing there is a reduction in alcoholic degree and a marked increase in aldehydes, formed from alcohols by oxidation, particularly acetaldehyde, so evident in the nose of *fino* sherries.

3 Both in biological and physico-chemical ageing, fusel oils (or higher alcohols, such as iso-butanol and iso-amyl alcohol) are formed.

4 While the layer of yeasts is forming on the surface of the wine, the glycerine content is reduced; with the establishment of the *flor*, the subsequent reduction is slower.

A great deal of work remains to be done to establish the exact mechanism by which the enzymes, or natural catalysts, in the yeasts bring about these complex chemical changes. Even some of the illustrious Masters of Wine totally misunderstand the process. Thus, one who shall be nameless misinforms readers that *fino* 'has spent its upbringing so protected from even a whiff of oxygen that it doesn't know how to react in its presence and succumbs to its oxidising charms in a flash.' In actual fact, the yeasts are living organisms which feed on constituents of the wine, but can do so only in the presence of oxygen, acting rather in the fashion of a semi-permeable membrane and allowing controlled access of oxygen – which also, of course, in limited amount, enters the cask, not only through the loosely stoppered bung-hole but through the pores of the wood. As the authoritative Manuel González Gordon has put it: 'It is a fact that sherry keeps extremely well on ullage, even when in bottle, and one of the reasons is probably that it is matured in full contact with air. Experience has shown that Sherry is very stable, although the causes are really not very clear.'

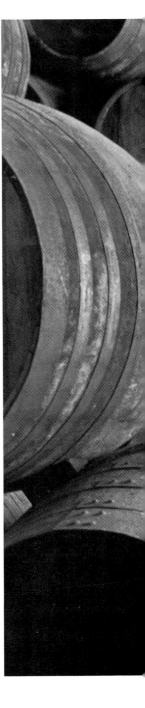

THE SOLERA SYSTEM

22 Amontillado
solera at Antonio
Barbadillo in Sanlúcar
de Barrameda

Wines are usually wood-aged by leaving them in the same cask –
except in so far as the contents are racked off the lees and transferred
as a whole to a fresh cask. This is known technically as static ageing;

the dynamic ageing or fractional blending of sherry in a *solera* is entirely different and involves a mixing process in which there is a partial withdrawal of sherry with a corresponding replacement of younger wine.

How the system works can best be explained by a simple example. At the start the *solera* might consist of one to a hundred butts of a four-year-old wine, and similar numbers of butts of three-year-old, two-year-old and one-year-old sherry of the same type. This would be a *solera* of four 'scales'. The first containing the oldest wine, which is always at ground level, is the *solera* proper (the word comes from the Latin *solum*, meaning 'floor') and the other three are known as *criaderas* (from the Spanish word for 'nursery') and are numbered '2', '3' and '4'. The second and third scales are stacked on top of the first, and sometimes a fourth – though this depends upon the condition of the butts, as the weight may damage those in the bottom row. The *solera* may very well contain more than four scales – some of those in Sanlúcar de Barrameda run to as many as fourteen – in which case the butts are stacked separately, but in similar fashion, each scale occupying a horizontal row of butts. The scales are not always arranged in order of age, nor do all the scales in a stack of butts necessarily belong to the same *solera*, since it has been found that *fino* matures best when the butts are on the bottom or second tier, where conditions are cooler and more humid, while *oloroso* does well in the third tier.

When wine is required for bottling or blending, the same amount (from 5 to 40 per cent, depending upon the type of wine and number of scales in the *solera*) is withdrawn from each of the oldest butts. They are then replenished from the next in age (i.e. *criadera* 2) and these are made good with wine from *criadera* 3, and so on to the end of the series. The youngest butts are then topped up with young *añada* (vintage) wine of the same type.

Wine is drawn from a *fino solera* at more frequent intervals – usually twice or three times a year – than from *amontillado* or *oloroso soleras*. This is because it must be kept moving, otherwise the *flor* may thin out or die, thus altering the character of the wine. The *Reglamento* (see page 40) lays down that wine removed from the *solera* for bottling must be at least three years old, manifestly something which it is impossible for the Consejo Regulador to check except by organoleptic tests and by keeping strict records of the movement of wine through each bodega.

The process of removing wine from the *solera* and 'refreshing' it and all the *criaderas* in turn is known as 'working the scales'. This was traditionally done by hand with a set of special and picturesque-looking utensils, and there are bodegas, such as Valdespino, which to this day will not hear of anything else. To avoid disturbance, wine is removed from a butt with a siphon, its end well below the *flor*, and collected in a pitcher (*jarra*) holding one *arroba* or one-thirtieth of a shipping butt of 500 litres. Again, when making up the contents of a butt with younger wine, it is poured into a large wedge-shape funnel (*canoa*) and introduced below the level of the *flor* through a long perforated tube (*rociador*). The wine removed from one butt is not all poured into one other, but distributed between a number so as to avoid variations as between different butts. The time and labour involved in this manual process has made it impracticable in the large bodegas, where methods have been developed using pumps and plastic hoses without disturbance to the wine.

The whole process is feasible only because in limited admixture, younger wines rapidly take on the character of the older. It is at once evident that with the *solera* system, which ensures the maintenance of style and quality year in and year out, there are no vintage wines. However, individual bodegas, notably Williams & Humbert, do as a matter of interest keep comprehensive 'libraries' of vintage sherries or *añadas*.

Once set up, a fractional blending system becomes more and more valuable with the passage of time as the average age of the wine in the older barrels increases, and there are examples in Jerez of *soleras* set up a hundred years ago or more, which, because only a proportion of the wine in the oldest butts is ever removed, still contain a minute amount of the wine originally laid down. That wine of this age, even in tiny amount is extraordinarily potent in its ability to affect the flavour is vividly illustrated by a demonstration carried out for visitors at the El Molino bodega of Pedro Domecq. Among other ancient butts is a 240-year-old 'Napoleon' so concentrated in flavour as to be undrinkable. If a little of the black fluid is swirled around a *copita* and then returned to the butt, and fresh 'La Ina' is poured into the same glass, the result is to transform it into something with the colour, nose and flavour, if not the body, of an old *oloroso*.

In what is regarded in the United States as the definitive book on Spanish cooking and wines, I was astonished to come across the statement that 'sherry, contrary to table wines, will be exposed to air and light in vast sun-filled naves.' It was Richard Ford, in his *Gatherings from Spain* of 1846, who first compared the sherry bodegas to cathedrals, and his description of them and their organisation is a great deal more accurate than the American 1985 version and impossible to better:

23 *Don José Ignacio Domecq, 'The Nose', most famous of sherry tasters*

These temples of Bacchus resemble cathedrals in size and loftiness, and their divisions, like Spanish chapels, bear the names of the saints to whom they are dedicated . . . [The] huge repositaries are all above ground, and are the antithesis of our under-ground cellars . . . As these wines are more capricious in their development than young ladies at boarding school, the greatest care is taken in the selection of eligible and healthy situations for their education . . . The interior of the *bodega* is kept deliciously cool; the glare outside is carefully excluded, while a free circulation of air is admitted; and even temperature is very essential, and one at an average temperature of 60 degrees is the best of all.

One result of housing the *soleras* in dry, airy bodegas above ground is that, in contrast to table wines, which are aged in cellars with a high relative humidity and where there is a preferential transpiration and evaporation of alcohol through the pores of the cask, in Jerez it is the other way round. Water is lost through the pores of the wood in preference to alcohol, and this explains the steady rise in alcoholic strength of old *olorosos* (of up to 24°) kept in wood for very long periods.

A personage of the greatest importance in the day-to-day running of a bodega is the *capataz* or head cellarman. Although circumstances have changed in some respects, Ford's description of the breed is too good to omit:

24 Don José Ignacio Domecq Jr. pouring with a venencia

> The rearing, educating, and finishing, as it were, of these wines, is a work of many years and is entrusted to the *Capataz* . . .
> These Highlanders are celebrated for the length of their pedigrees, and

the tasting properties of their tongues; we have more than once in
Estremadura and Leon fallen in with flights of these ragged gentry,
wending, Scotch-like, to the south in search of fortune . . .

These gentlemen of good birth and better taste seldom smoke, as the
narcotic stupifying weed deadens papillatory delicacy. Now as few wine-
masters in Spain would give up the cigar to gain millions, the *Capataz* soon
becomes the sole possessor of the secrets of the cellar . . .

Times have, of course, changed, and nowadays the making of the
wines is under constant supervision from a qualified oenologist, backed
up by a laboratory with the latest in modern analytical and
investigative apparatus. Nevertheless, apart from overseeing the day-to-
day operations in the bodega, the *capataz* still fulfils a key role in
regularly tasting each butt of wine in his care. Ford compares him with
a schoolmaster:

> He goes the regular round of his butts, ascertaining the qualities, merits
> and demerits of each pupil, which he notes by certain marks of
> hieroglyphs. He corrects faults as he goes along, making also a
> memorandum of the date and remedy applied, and thus at his next visit is
> enabled to report good progress or lament the contrary.

The instrument with which the *capataz* takes samples is the *venencia*.
In its simplest and earliest form, as used in Sanlúcar de Barrameda, this
consists of a long piece of bamboo, cut so that the lower end forms a
small cup with a knot of the cane at the bottom. This is plunged
smoothly into the wine so as to disturb the layer of *flor* as little as
possible. In Jerez the design is more sophisticated, the cup being made
of silver or stainless steel and mounted on a long, springy whalebone
handle with a hook at the top – both to hang it up and to prevent it
slipping accidentally into the butt. It is anything but easy for the
amateur to use a *venencia*, but a cellarman in Jerez will in one hand
hold half-a-dozen *copitas* at waist level and with the other pour a little
sherry into each of them with a *venencia* held above his head. This has
indeed become a ritual when parties of visitors are shown around the
bodegas, with the *capataz* dressed for the occasion in a smart red jacket
with a silk sash.

Oddly enough the *venencia* is not Spanish, but Greek in origin and
was used in Homeric times for extracting wine from amphorae, as was
pointed out by H. Warner Allen in his *History of Wine*. In his book he
reproduces the picture of a cup-bearer with a *venencia* exactly similar in
appearance to those used in Jerez today, as portrayed on a beaker
dating from c. 490 BC.

BLENDING AND BOTTLING

A few of the best *finos* and *amontillados* on sale to the public are straight *solera* wines, but this is the exception rather than the rule, firstly because such wines are expensive and secondly because they are bone-dry, and the largest market is for sweeter wines. (The house of Emilio Lustau is to be congratulated on introducing a range of unblended *almacenista* sherries, which have delighted connoisseurs on both sides of the Atlantic.) Apérítif wines apart, there is the range of dessert *olorosos*, cream sherries and pale cream sherries, all of which are made by blending dry wine from the *solera* with one of a number of different sweetening wines.

25 Control panel of refrigeration plant at Luís Caballero

The best *finos* are taken straight from the *solera* and untreated apart from clarification and refrigeration to throw potassium bitartrate (see page 77). In the past, wines for export were slightly fortified to bring them up to 17° of alcohol, but EEC regulations now permit them to be shipped with only 15·5°. This poses its own problems in the case of *finos* shipped in bulk in containers, since the low degree of alcohol renders them more liable to attack by micro-organisms, and very strict hygiene and the use of micro-filters is necessary. Less expensive *finos* are often blended with cheaper wine from Chiclana and a little *manzanilla* is added to improve the nose. Some of the best *finos* and *manzanillas* are very slightly sweetened, but this must be done with *dulce de almíbar* (see page 76) to avoid spoiling and darkening them.

Genuine *amontillado* is necessarily very expensive, since the starting point is an old *fino* which is matured further without *flor*, involving in all a minimum eight years of ageing. The cheaper wines sold as such contain only a very limited amount of the real article and are much less concentrated in nose and flavour. In his *Sherry* (third edition, London, 1982), Julian Jeffs gives the *cabaceo* or recipe for a typical commercial *amontillado* as follows:

Fino fuerte	Ro (= 13·5@)
Amontillado Dolores	5@
MZA *Puro*	2@
Vino Chiclana *Fino*	7@
Dulce	2·5@
	———
	30@

In this example, the quantities are given in *arrobas*, thirty *arrobas* making up a standard shipping butt; Ro stands for *resto* (or 'remainder'), in this case 13·5 *arrobas*. MZA stands for *manzanilla* and *Dolores* refers to sweetening wine, so that the only *amontillado* in this blend is the 16·7 per cent of *amontillado Dulce* – which is, in fact, itself a blend containing only about half *amontillado*.

'Medium' sherry is not a term that appears in the *Reglamento* of the Consejo Regulador and is used to describe *olorosos* and wines of the '*amontillado*' type that have been somewhat sweetened with *vino dulce*, corresponding to what the Spanish call *abocados* or semi-sweet wines. They are complicated blends with as many as a dozen or fifteen different ingredients, but, as they are usually very moderately priced, will not contain much real *amontillado*.

The basis of the cream sherries (see also Chapter 6) is always a dry *solera* wine: *oloroso* in the case of the traditional dark and rich dessert wines; and *fino*, perhaps with a little pale *amontillado* to give it more body, for the pale creams, more recently introduced. A variety of wines may be used for sweetening the dry base wine.

The traditional sweetening wine in Jerez is the dark Pedro Ximénez or PX, which is also drunk in its own right as a dessert wine. It is made from the grapes of the same name by sunning them on esparto grass mats, so concentrating the sugar to the extent that some of it is

26 Filtration plant and stainless steel storage tanks at Croft's

left in the wine when fermentation ends. To make an even sweeter wine for blending, fermentation is cut short by adding grape spirit to the must, so curtailing fermentation and resulting in an intensely sweet *mistela*. Similar wines may be made in the same way from Moscatel grapes; aged in *solera*, they are intensely sweet and fragrant and, like the PX wines, are among the bodegas' most valuable assets.

Pedro Ximénez is, however, decreasingly grown in the demarcated sherry region. In the past the sherry houses relied on PX from the neighbouring region of Montilla–Moriles, where the Pedro Ximénez is the predominant grape. Importation became more difficult when Montilla–Moriles became a *denominación de origen* in its own right, but continued to a limited extent; whether, with tough new EEC regulations coming into effect, this will still be countenanced remains to be seen.

Another sweetening wine 'imported' from Los Palacios, and from Huelva and Montilla outside the region, was *dulce apagado*. It was a cheaper wine made from a variety of grapes and brandied before fermentation so as to make a *mistela* in the fashion described for PX.

Now that the sherry producers are being forced back on their own resources, PX is largely being replaced for sweetening by *dulce pasa*, a wine made in exactly the same way by sunning the grapes and adding grape spirit to the must, but from good quality Palomino. It is proving a very acceptable alternative.

The dark colour and intense flavour of sweetening wines of the PX type are an asset in making the traditional dessert wines, such as 'Bristol Cream'. However, for adding a touch of sweetness to *finos* or for making the increasingly popular pale creams, a sweetening agent as near as possible colourless and without nose or flavour of its own is required.

One such wine is *dulce de almíbar* made by dissolving pure invert sugar (a 50/50 mixture of glucose and fructose, similar to the sugars occurring naturally in grape) in *fino* and leaving the blend to mature. However, in certain European countries it is not permitted to add sugar to wine except to chaptalised table wines, where the sugar is added to the must before fermentation. The use of *dulce de almíbar* is therefore limited – though the purpose of a ban on adding natural sugar in small amount to sherry seems obscure.

In making 'Croft Original', the biggest-selling of the pale cream sherries, Croft's use a concentrated or 'rectified' must for sweetening. This is grape juice (the type of grape is immaterial) which is concentrated until it contains 33 per cent of sugar and then decolourised with activated charcoal.

Another type of wine prepared for blending with sherries is *vino de color*. This is used to darken the colour of styles such as 'Old East India' and brown sherry. According to H. Warner Allen, the practice of boiling down must to give body and sweetness to wines dates from Greek and Roman times, and the *defrutum* and *sapa* of the Romans, syrups made by reducing the wine to a third and a half of its original volume, would seem to correspond closely to the *sancocho* and *arrope* made in Jerez today. They are prepared, as are similar syrups in Málaga, by simmering the must in a copper cauldron over a slow wood fire for periods of up to twenty hours. Two parts of the dark syrup are then mixed with straight must and fermented. As *vino de color* matures, it develops great depth of nose and toffee-like flavour, and the old wine is very valuable.

As drawn from the *solera*, the wines are slightly turbid. A bright appearance in the glass adds to the attraction of a sherry – and, in fact, a sherry that is slightly cloudy, but in other more important respects perfect, may be rejected by the uninstructed consumer. The wine is therefore clarified before being bottled. This was traditionally done with egg white, the whites of egg being beaten up with a whisk of thyme branches into a little of the wine to be clarified and then poured into the butt and stirred with a rod known as an *apaleador*. The albumen attracted to itself the suspended colloidal particles, and clarification was completed by adding Spanish earth, a fine-grained clay from Lebrija in the north of the sherry region, which carried down to the bottom of the butt all the albumen and any other suspended matter. The unwanted egg yolks were, incidentally, the perquisite of the *capataz* and were sold by him to the confectioners or to the nuns for making, together with almonds, the Moorish-style sweetmeats so typical of Andalucía.

This process is still used in the medium-sized and smaller bodegas where operations are still mainly carried out by hand. In the large mechanised bodegas the wine is clarified by filtration. A further contingency is the separation of crystals of cream of tartar (or potassium bitartrate) in cold weather. Tartar is a perfectly natural constituent of wine and its appearance in bottle has no adverse effects, but often worries the purchaser. To ensure that the wine remains clear in all circumstances it is first centrifuged and then refrigerated to $-8°C$ to precipitate the crystals. In the past it would be kept at very low temperature, but without of course freezing it, for about a week, but it has now been found that by seeding the cold wine precipitation occurs immediately. The crystals are removed by filtering the wine through kieselguhr or cellulose micro-filters.

CHAPTER 6

Enjoying Sherry

THE DIFFERENT STYLES

It is probably still true to say that no two casks of young sherry mature in exactly the same way. If left to its own devices, the wine usually intensifies in character, but there are rogue butts which change style completely – though there are not likely to be drastic changes after three years.

Together with *manzanilla*, the *Reglamento* (see page 41) defines five basic types of sherry according to the characteristics of the must and the method of maturing the wine. They are *fino, amontillado, oloroso, palo cortado* and *raya*. There are, however, numerous subdivisions, and the simplest approach is to bear in mind the major divide – between wines that grow a plentiful *flor* (i.e. *fino* and *manzanilla*) and those that do not (i.e. *oloroso* and *palo cortado*). *Amontillado* originates from a *fino*, but develops further without the protection of *flor*, and the relationship between the different styles may conveniently be shown by the diagram overleaf.

All these basic types as drawn from the *solera* are completely dry, and sweetened sherries, such as medium, pale cream, cream and brown are made by blending them with the different varieties of *vino*

27 Palomino grapes and copitas *of sherry*

dulce and, where deeper colour is required, with *vino de color* (see pages 75–77).

The official definition of the *Reglamento* is quoted at or near the beginning of each of the following notes.

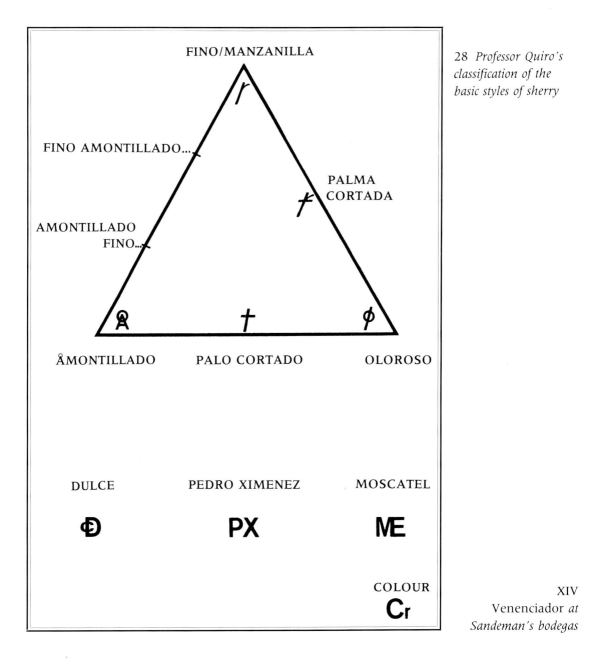

28 Professor Quiro's classification of the basic styles of sherry

XIV
Venenciador *at Sandeman's bodegas*

XV
*A prince among
tasters: Don José Ignacio
Domecq*

XVI
*Different styles of sherry:
From left to right:*
fino, *pale cream,*
amontillado,
palo cortado, oloroso,
Pedro Ximénez

Fino

'A pale straw-coloured wine with pungent yet delicate bouquet (of almonds), light, dry and with little acidity and containing 15·5° to 17° of alcohol (percentage by volume).'

Fino is slightly fortified for shipment and sometimes very slightly sweetened, but otherwise contains no additives or wine other than Palomino matured under *flor*. A recent tasting panel saw fit to explain that caramel 'is used to bolster the wine and give it structure and will also soften it and make it rounder.' The idea of adding caramel to one of the palest and driest of wines like *fino* is so ludicrous that one can only think that the panel member was confusing it with Jerez brandy. Again, as to the imagined nosings of Moscatel in *finos* by this same panel, it should be pointed out that any shipper guilty of such a practice would be most severely disciplined, or even suspended, under Articles 5° and 48° to 59° of the *Reglamento*.

Top class *fino* sherries that are particularly clean and delicate in nose are known as *palmas*, and are labelled *uno, dos, tres* and *cuatro palmas* according to age. The term *palma cortado*, on the other hand, denotes a more robust *fino* tending towards *amontillado*, while wines of the *fino* type lacking in delicacy are called *entre-finos*.

With prolonged age in cask (but *not* in bottle – see page 66), *finos* may develop in various ways. The rare old *fino*, matured in this way, is a superb wine. What is more likely, as the *flor* thins and finally dies, is that the wine will gain body and a new intensity of nose and flavour, developing first into a *fino amontillado* and then into *amontillado*.

Fino and light *amontillado* are the basis for pale cream sherry, which is made by sweetening them (see below).

Amontillado

Amontillado takes its name from the neighbouring region of Montilla, where wines similar in general type to sherry are made by the *solera* system. It is defined by the *Reglamento* as 'An amber-coloured wine with pungent and nutty (hazelnut) aroma, smooth and full on the palate, dry with an alcohol content of between 18° and 20°.' This hardly conveys the intensity of nose and flavour of a good *amontillado*. It was Manuel M. González Gordon who first compared the bouquets of *fino, amontillado* and *oloroso* to almonds, hazelnuts and walnuts. I feel that, while almonds very well decibe a *fino*, hazelnuts hardly do justice to a splendidly rich and aromatic *amontillado*, savoury, a touch phenolic and very slightly sweet at the same time, with a hint of Armagnac – shut your eyes and you could be among the butts in Jerez in the heart of one of the great bodegas. Not without justice did Chaucer write:

This wine of Spain creepeth subtilly
In other wines, growing fast by,
Of which there riseth such fumositee,
That when a man hath drunken draughtes three,
And weeneth that he be at home in Chepe,
He is in Spain, right at the town of Lepe,
Nor at the Rochelle, nor at Bordeaux town.

As already explained, *amontillado* originates from further maturation of *fino* in the absence of *flor*. This is an oxidative process resulting in the deepening of colour, which becomes even darker than amber with age, and the enhancement of nose and flavour. Since the youngest *amontillado* is at least eight years old, the genuine article is necessarily expensive, and it is regrettable that much of the '*amontillado*' sold abroad is a confected blend made to imitate it.

Oloroso

The name is derived from a Spanish word meaning 'fragrant' or 'sweet-smelling', and it is officially defined as 'A dark-golden wine, very aromatic as the name indicates, full-bodied and reminiscent of walnuts, dry or very slightly sweet, with an alcohol content of between 18° and 20°.' In fact, old *olorosos* may approach 24° (per cent by volume) of alcohol through preferential transpiration of water through the walls of the butt (see page 71) and become almost black in colour.

Olorosos, as already noted (page 64), are wines developing little *flor*, which is killed by fortification, after which the wines are matured by a purely physico-chemical, oxidative process. When young, they are only light brown in colour, but darken and gain body and a more maderised nose and flavour with further ageing. In their natural state they are completely dry – except for a very slightly sweet finish caused by traces of glycerine. A clean young *oloroso* such as Pedro Domecq's justly renowned 'Río Viejo' is an ideal winter apéritif in cold climes such as those of Scotland – as the author can testify from personal experience!

The older and darker *olorosos* are often blended with Pedro Ximénez or other sweetening wines and with *vino de color* to make sweet dessert sherries. (See below: Cream sherry (including *amoroso*), Brown sherry and East India sherry.)

Palo Cortado

'A type of wine intermediate between the two foregoing, with the aroma of *amontillado* and the colour and palate or *oloroso*, and with alcoholic degree similar to it.' *Palo cortado* is a rare and choice wine with intense nose and flavour, but relatively little of it has been made since the phylloxera epidemic, and a *solera* of *palo cortado* is difficult to operate, since there is a tendency for the wine to degenerate into *oloroso*. According to age it is labelled *uno*, *dos*, *tres*, and *cuatro cortados*. Because of its rarity and costliness, there is a temptation to concoct *palo cortado* by blending *amontillado* and *oloroso*, so that one should be careful that it has been shipped by a really reliable firm.

Raya

'A wine with characteristics similar to *oloroso*, but with a less delicate aroma.' The wines, of which you will often see the butts maturing in the open air, are coarser and not as clean on the nose as *oloroso*. The better are known as *rayas olorosos* and the lighter as *rayas finas*.

Manzanilla

'The wine covered by the Denominación de Origen "Manzanilla–Sanlúcar de Barrameda" and traditionally known as *manzanilla*. It is a *fino*-style wine, very pale in colour, characteristically pungent, light on the palate, dry and only slightly acidic, and with an alcohol content of between 15·5° and 17°. Its special characteristics result from the process of ageing under *flor* in the bodegas of the specified *zona de crianza*.'

There are various theories as to the origin of the name, the most likely being an imagined similarity in taste to that of camomile tea, similarly named in Spanish. I do remember asking for *manzanilla* in one of the many *tabernas* of the Calle Ventura de la Vega in Madrid and being given a cup of the tea – which was light and aromatic enough, but not exactly to my taste on a sweltering August afternoon! To add to the confusion there is a type of large green olive called *manzanilla*, and in his *Sherry* Julian Jeffs tells a very amusing story about a well-known shipper who sent a small barrel of them to one of his English customers as a Christmas present – only to receive the puzzled comment that someone had tampered with the wine, which 'tasted strongly of salt and was full of foreign bodies'.

Some of the differences between making *manzanilla* and a *fino* from Jerez have been touched on in Chapter 5. In the first place, the grapes are picked about a week earlier than around Jerez, while not quite ripe and containing rather more malic acid. Owing to the prevailing breeze from the sea, greater humidity and more uniform temperatures, the *flor* grows thickly all the year round, and the operation of the *soleras* is somewhat different. There are more 'scales' (see page 68), usually nine to fourteen, and the wine is moved from scale to scale more rapidly. In Jerez it is usual to draw off wine from the *solera* twice a year, while in

Sanlúcar smaller amounts are withdrawn every few months. To avoid disturbance to the *flor*, when refreshing a butt with younger wine, it is added through a *garceta* or finely textured hessian sack, rather than the perforated *rociador* used in Jerez.

The special character of *manzanilla* derives more from the manner and place in which it is matured than from the character of the must. Much of the must used for making *manzanilla* in fact comes from vineyards around Jerez, and a butt of must from Jerez will develop as *manzanilla* if taken to one of the bodegas of Sanlúcar de Barrameda for maturation; if, on the other hand, must from the Sanlúcar area is taken to Jerez it will develop as normal sherry.

The typical form of *manzanilla*, *fina*, corresponds to the *fino* from Jerez, but is lighter, saltier in flavour and faintly bitter in finish, with its own very delicate *flor*-type nose; it tastes at its best on the spot, drunk as an apéritif or with the wonderful seafood from the Bay of Cádiz, or in hot weather anywhere. When *manzanilla fina* ages and loses its *flor*, it then matures in the manner of an *amontillado*, turning first into *manzanilla pasada*, corresponding to a *fino-amontillado*, and later to *manzanilla amontillada* with a yet deeper amber colour, more body and alcohol content of up to 20°.

Medium Sherry

This is a description applied to light *amontillados* and *olorosos*, which have been somewhat sweetened. It is a fact that, purists apart, most sherry-drinkers in the northern climes where the bulk of the wine is drunk prefer a touch of sweetness in it – hence the success of the big-selling 'Dry Sack', which its makers are currently advertising as 'About as dry as . . . a day's cricket at Old Trafford or tennis at Wimbledon.' This shrewdly invokes the snob appeal of a supposedly dry wine with a broad hint that it is anything but that. It is in fact a very smooth, good quality *amontillado*, sweetened, but not overpoweringly so. Many other inexpensive medium *amontillados* are not straight blends of *amontillado* with sweetening wine, but rather a complex mixture made up to sell at a price and containing only a modicum of actual *amontillado* (see page 74).

Pale Cream

Pale Cream did not exist before 1970, when in the form of 'Croft Original' it was launched on the British market, where this new style of wine now accounts for 25 per cent of sherry sales. It has proved highly successful in other foreign markets and most of the major bodegas now have their own brand. It is made by blending *fino* and light *amontillado* with concentrated and decolourised must, as described on page 76. It is notorious that the public in general likes sweet wines, and the appeal of the pale creams is that they are not overpoweringly sweet, light enough to be drunk as an apéritif, yet with sufficient body and flavour to do duty at other times – much in the way of the Verdelho madeira, before it became too expensive, among generations of more sophisticated drinkers.

Cream Sherry

'Cream' and 'Milk' sherries, denoting rich, sweetened *olorosos*, are a peculiarly British institution, originating in Bristol, with its long tradition of shipping wines, where two firms, Harvey's and Avery's, are particularly associated with them. Since Britain has always accounted for the lion's share of the sherry market, the Spanish houses have long ago followed suit with their own brands.

There is an amusing note on Bristol Milk and Bristol Cream in *Harveys of Bristol* by Thomas Henry:

> The 17th-century clergyman Thomas Fuller, writing in his *History of the Worthies of England*, has no doubt why the name Milk had been applied to the most famous brand of Bristol sherry.
>
> 'Some will have called it Milk,' he said, 'because such wine is the first moisture given to infants in this city.' Nearly a century-and-a-half later, the Prince of Wales, shortly to become Edward VII, was struck by much the same thought. 'All I can say is,' he said between sips, 'you must have dam' fine cows.' In 1949, with a humour that was no less acute for being unconscious, it was the turn of the Ministry of Food. In a letter dated December of that year it drew the attention of John Harvey & Sons to Regulation One of the Defence (Sales of Food) Regulations, 1943, which made it an offence to mislead the public about the nature or nutritional value of any food . . .
>
> The company's response was courteous, logical, and spiked with a restrained but gleeful wit. After pointing out that Bristol Milk had been in existence for somewhat longer than the Ministry of Food (300 years at least), it went on to presume that the same objection must logically apply to Bristol Cream and hence 'to all shaving creams, hair creams, face creams, boot creams, etc., as suggesting they have a nutritive value.'

Bristol Cream was, in fact, a much later introduction than Bristol Milk, the first recorded reference to it being in 1882. The name, it is said, was coined by an aristocratic lady visitor to Harvey's cellars in Denmark Street in the mid-nineteenth century. Persuaded to try it, she said, 'If that is the milk, then *this* must be the cream.' It is now the largest-selling sherry, both in Britain and in the world.

The making of cream dessert sherries by blending *oloroso* with a sweetening wine, such as Pedro Ximénez, and *vino de color* has already been described (page 75). In the case of 'Bristol Cream', the wine is shipped in nitrogen-capped containers to Shoreham in Sussex and then transported to Bristol for final blending and bottling.

There is, of course, a great variety of rich, raisiny, velvet-smooth old cream sherries, the quality depending on that of the *oloroso* and its age, also on that of the Pedro Ximénez and *vino de color*, both at their best extremely costly commodities. Unlike *fino* or *manzanilla*, good cream sherry actually improves in bottle as the sugar is consumed and it develops a bitter-sweet finish.

Another name used for smooth, sweet *olorosos* is *amoroso*, meaning 'loving' in Spanish, but in fact the name of a vineyard. Charming as it is, one does not nowadays often see the name, most such sherries being labelled as 'cream'.

Brown Sherry

This is a very dark, sweet and rich dessert sherry, containing a large amount of *raya* wine in addition to *oloroso*, *vino dulce* and *vino de color*. An extremely sweet version of this wine, known as *pajarete* or *paxarete*, is sometimes used in small amount to enhance the flavour and colour of cheap whisky.

East India Sherry

There is a Jerezano proverb which runs:

> Mareado el buen vino de Jarez
> Si valía cinco, vale diez.

> (Seasick, the good wine of Jerez
> is worth double.)

This refers to the old custom of carrying sherry to distant destinations in the holds of sailing ships in the interests of obtaining a smoother and more mature wine. The practice began with the vessels of the East India Company, and it seems that as early as 1617 English merchants in Surat were enjoying sack shipped out from England. As with madeira, the improvement was evidently caused by more rapid evaporation from the surface of the staves and the movement of the liquid against the walls of the cask, resulting in changes in internal pressure and increased transpiration of air through the pores.

I am indebted for this information to an extremely well-written pamphlet *Ben Line Old East India Sherry – A Background History*, produced by the proprietors of a Scottish shipping line whose vessels were still carrying butts of sherry early in the present century; one such was the *Romano–Benlarig–1904*, the *Benlarig* being a Ben Line steamship lost on Admiralty service in 1917. To continue in the words of the pamphlet:

> As sail gave way to steam the practice began to decline but throughout the nineteenth century Old East India sherry was a byword for excellence. Charles Dickens in *David Copperfield* tells how Mr Tiffey, the old clerk, visited Mr Spenlow at Norwood and was given 'brown East India sherry there, of a quality so precious as to make a man wink.' . . .
>
> It seemed a pity that such an ancient custom and one which had such rewarding results should entirely disappear, and they [the owners of the Ben Line] decided to revive it. Messrs Alistair Campbell, wine merchants of Edinburgh, expressed interest in the idea which was enthusiastically taken up by Messrs Wilson & Valdespino of Liverpool, London and Jerez. So it came about that in July 1958 a trial hogshead containing 54 gallons of Wilson & Valdespino's finest old dry Oloroso was shipped in *Benlomond* for a Far East round voyage of over 20,000 miles. On its return the hogshead was bottled, and before *Bendoran* sailed with a second hogshead a ceremonial tasting was held on board that vessel . . .
>
> At the tasting ceremony the sceptics were happily confounded. The sherry which had made the voyage was tasted against the same sherry which had not. It is of course difficult to improve on perfection and Wilson & Valdespino's 'Solera del 1847' by the time that it is ready for shipment is an unsurpassed wine of its type. Nevertheless the experts present at the tasting, who included no less an authority than Mr André Simon, were unanimous in deciding that the travelled sherry was not only smoother and rounder on the palate but had acquired a richer and brighter colour and a subtly enhanced bouquet.

KEEPING AND SERVING SHERRY

Sherry is probably more abused in the keeping and serving than any other wine. It is more or less general knowledge that bottles of table wine should be stored on their sides in a cool place so that the cork is in contact with the liquid and remains airtight, or again that light white wines are best served cool and reds at room temperature.

Sherry, on the other hand, often seems to be regarded as impervious to the most casual treatment. How often has one seen bottles of *fino* standing half-empty on the shelves of an overheated bar? This happens not only in Britain and the United States but also in Spain; outside Andalucía the consumption of sherry is lower than it is in the UK, so that in the hot Spanish summer the contents of such a bottle may well be undrinkable. Whatever one's favourite brand, smart tactics in such circumstances are to go for an unopened bottle and to refuse the end of an opened one. I remember an occasion in the Rioja, when I watched with incredulity as the barman poured the dregs of one bottle into a glass, opened a fresh one and was about to top up with it until I stopped him.

The reason why bottles of sherry are usually stored upright is that fortified wines are more apt to attack the corks than table wines. *Finos* and light *amontillados* are at their best when freshly bottled and should not be kept for more than three months, so that there is no advantage in binning the bottles on their sides. In sweetened form as Pale Cream the same wines will keep in good condition for two to three years. Choice old *olorosos* and cream sherries improve with bottle age as the sugar is gradually consumed, and if they are to be kept for long periods should be binned horizontally; in this case long corks of good quality, such as those used for vintage port, are necessary.

Visits to the bodegas in Jerez always end in a *salón de degustación*, cool and half-lit after the midday glare of Andalucía. Here it is the custom to serve *fino* chilled and from half-bottles. There is good reason for this, since, once a bottle of *fino* is opened it loses its fresh *flor* nose fairly rapidly. The famous Professor Saintsbury claimed to detect a difference between lunch and dinner, but three days is probably nearer the mark for those with less acute sensibilities, and if the bottle is recorked and kept in the door of the fridge it should remain in good condition for at least a week (wines of any sort will, of course, keep fresh for much longer in a refrigerator, for the good reason that the rate of oxidation, like that of all chemical changes, doubles for each 10°C rise in temperature). Julian Jeffs makes the sensible suggestion that if the whole contents of a bottle of *fino* are not to be consumed for some time, half should be poured off into a clean half-bottle and tightly corked.

Another failing of the service of *fino* sherry in many bars and restaurants is that it is poured lukewarm and brimful into the wrong type of glass. The ideal glass for any type of sherry is the tall *copita* tapering towards the top, which should be not more than half filled so as to concentrate all the aromatic fragrance of the wine. The worst possible type is the small 'sherry' glass used in most bars, rather wider at the top than the bottom. If used as a measure (albeit a thimbleful) and filled full, it is almost impossible to nose even the most fragrant of wines. If faced with this situation, ask for the contents to be poured into a tulip shaped wine glass or a brandy glass and add an ice cube to the *fino* if really necessary (but this can be overdone. At Rockefeller Center in New York, I was recently served 'Tío Pepe' both on the rocks and with twists of lemon peel. There *is* a sherry, Harvey's 'Tico', which is specially blended for use with mixers and ice).

Of the styles of sherry other than *fino* and *manzanilla*, I prefer to drink a light *amontillado* slightly cooled and the others at room temperature; and the proper glass, only a third to half full, enormously improves any of them. The stouter and sweeter sherries will keep for at least a month or two in an opened bottle.

As to the choice of a style of sherry for a particular occasion, I hesitate to pontificate – for example, I know of people who enjoy drinking a well-known cream sherry before meals. *Salud*, as they say in Spain, though it is not something I would do myself (the point being that wines containing much sugar tend to satisfy the appetite rather than stimulate it). It is, of course, usual to drink a *fino* or light *amontillado* before food; in cold weather I prefer the rather fuller-bodied dry *oloroso* or *palo cortado*. A further consideration is the wine

29 The end of the visit: sampling sherry at the bodegas of Pedro Domecq

that is to follow at table. A full-blooded *amontillado* swamps most of the new-style light and fruity cold-fermented white wines; on the other hand, there are acidic white wines which are too similar to *fino* to follow it pleasurably, and in such cases it seems better to go for a contrast and start with *amontillado*.

The old *olorosos* and cream sherries come into their own after a meal, when they make an attractive alternative to port – and it has justly been said that sherry sits much better on champagne than port.

SHERRY WITH FOOD

Outside Andalucía, sherry is normally drunk either as an apéritif before a meal or as a dessert wine at the end. In Jerez itself it is customary to drink chilled *fino* throughout a meal in place of a beverage wine, just as in Sanlúcar they accompany food with *manzanilla*, and in Córdoba with *montilla*. No doubt one reason is that it goes so well with the marvellous seafood from the Bay of Cádiz (see also Chapter 8). It also seems possible to drink a great deal more sherry in Jerez itself without ill effects than elsewhere; this would appear to have more to do with the climate than the fact that it is very slightly fortified for shipment abroad (and for the record, a light *fino* at 15·5° is not so much stronger than one of the more robust Californian Chardonnays).

Nearer home, it goes without saying that sherry is about the only wine to drink with soup, and among the perfect partnerings of wine with food I still, many years later, remember splitting a fresh half-bottle of La Riva 'Tres Palmas' with Hugh Johnson with oysters. However, between the different styles of sherry, there is such a range of flavours that proposals for matching them to the different courses of a full meal are hardly surprising. Professor Saintsbury did, in fact, try just this, and his suggestions were: 'Manzanilla with oysters. Montilla with soup and fish; and Amontillado with entrées and roast; an Amoroso or some such wine with sweets and for after dinner, the oldest and browners of "old Browns".'

To mark its fiftieth anniversary in October 1985 the Consejo Regulador held a conference in Jerez de la Frontera under the title of *Cita del Jerez y la Mesa* ('Sherry with Food'), to which it invited restaurateurs, wine-makers, and wine and food writers, both from Spain and abroad to discuss sherry as an accompaniment to food. For lunch and dinner each day we were invited by one or other of the bodegas to a meal specially devised to be accompanied by sherry and nothing else. I reproduce two of the menus, the first cooked for González Byass by Lalo Grosso de Macpherson, who bears the titles of 'Cocinera de Jerez' and 'Cocinera del Rey', and the second prepared for Pedro Domecq by Paul Schiff, the gifted chef and proprietor of La Hacienda in Marbella, one of the most sophisticated restaurants in Spain:

Lunch offered by González Byass at the Viña Las Canarias,
10 October 1985

Crema de calabaza al vinagre de Jerez
(Cream of squash with sherry vinegar)

Jerez fino

—

Urta asada al amontillado con verduras naturales
(Roast *urta* [see page 107] with *amontillado* and fresh vegetables)

Jerez amontillado

—

Solomillo al oloroso con guarnición de arroz y maíz
(Fillet steak with sherry garnished with rice and sweetcorn)

Jerez oloroso

—

Cocktail de melón, al Jerez
(Melon cocktail with sherry)

Jerez cream

—

Tarta de kiwi, al brandy
(Kiwi tart with brandy)

Jerez brandy

*Lunch offered by Pedro Domecq at the Palacio Domecq,
11 October 1985*

Pez de espada macerado con limón confitado
(Marinated swordfish with crystallised lemon)

Jerez fino

—

*Blinis de maíz con coquinas y albahaca
salsa al Jerez fino*
(Cornmeal blinis with cockles and fennel
and *fino* sauce)

Jerez amontillado

—

*Escalopes de patos con higos,
salsa agridulce de Jerez oloroso,
gratín de patatas*
(Scallops of duck with figs, sweet and sour *oloroso*
sauce and potatoes *au gratin*)

Jerez oloroso

—

*Helado montado al Solera
Sabañón frío
Frambuesas*
(Ice cream whipped with sherry
Chilled Zabaglione
Fresh raspberries)

Jerez cream

—

Jerez brandy

After sampling these and other gastronomic menus offered by Luís Caballero, in the picture book surroundings of the Moorish Castle of San Marcos in Puerto de Santa María, and by Antonio Barbadillo in Sanlúcar de Barrameda, the considered opinion of the delegates was that, while the chosen sherries perfectly complemented the individual dishes, it was an *embarras de richesses* to serve nothing but sherries throughout an entire meal and the same basic sherry flavour proved to be too repetitive. Speaking for myself, I also felt that the wines, apart from the *fino*, were too strong to drink freely with the food and found myself swigging iced water to slake my thirst. I confess that with meals in Jerez I do find myself hankering for a bottle of Rioja or Penedès – though the Jerezanos themselves are now making white table wines from the Palomino grape, notably the 'Castillo de San Diego' from Barbadillo, which are light, clean and refreshing though lacking somewhat in acidity.

The use of sherry in cooking and the regional cuisine of the sherry region are discussed in Chapter 8.

CHAPTER 7

Jerez Brandy

ORIGINS OF JEREZ BRANDY

It will probably come as a surprise to most readers that Spain is by far the largest producer of brandy in the world. Most of it is made in Jerez de la Frontera by the sherry firms, and at times of crisis in the sherry trade sales of brandy at home and in South America have been the saving of more than one of the leading concerns. In Britain and the United States the trade and wine writers have assiduously fostered the idea that the only brandies worth drinking are *cognac* and *armagnac*; but as Nicholas Faith, writing in *Gourmetour*, has well put it, Spanish brandies 'do all offer an alternative range of experiences to their French rivals. They are almost invariably, warmer, richer, fuller and, in many cases, deliberately sweeter . . . [with] an unmistakable velvetiness of their own on the palate as well as on the nose.'

Thanks to the Moorish invasion and the work of the twelfth-century Toledan school of translators, the art of distillation, which the Arabs had learnt from pioneers such as Zosimos of Panoplis in the third or fourth century AD, was familiar in Spain long before the rest of Western Europe. The words *alambique* (Spanish for a 'still' or 'alembic') and 'alcohol' itself are both of Arabic origin. The first practical use for alcohol, attributed to the thirteenth-century Spanish doctor and alchemist, Arnold of Vilanova, was for medicinal purposes; in Jerez, the practice of distilling grape spirit for the fortification of wine was well-established during the sixteenth century – at about the time the Charentais were distilling the first *cognac*. In 1833 Cyrus Redding wrote

30 One of the oldest copper brandy stills in Jerez, in the bodegas of Valdespino

95

in his *A History and Description of Modern Wines* of the high quality of the Spanish spirit; Catalan brandy was exported as early as the seventeenth century in response to a demand from England, but in Jerez brandy was not marketed commercially until the late nineteenth century.

One of the pioneers was Pedro Domecq Loustau of the famous sherry house. During the nineteenth century the firm, like others, was engaged in shipping grape spirit to Holland. Known as *holandas*, as it still is, it was used by the Dutch for making liqueurs. In 1850, Domecq were late in delivering a large consignment; it was refused by the Amsterdam importer and they were left with it on their hands. It remained in oak casks, and when some years later Don Pedro tasted it, he was so struck by its quality that he elaborated it as brandy. This was the origin of the well-known 'Fundador', first sold to the public in 1874. Another Jerezano who had much to do with the establishment of the trade was Francisco Ivison O'Neale, who by 1880 was maturing large stocks of brandy along Charentais lines and shrewdly shipping it to England under the name of 'La Marque Spéciale', without mention of Jerez or of his firm, F.G. Cosens & Co.

At the time when the Jerezanos began bottling brandy there was no international agreement on labelling, and the name *coñac* was introduced to describe it. According to Manuel M. González Gordon, the word first appeared in print in 1853 and was incorporated in the fourteenth edition of the *Diccionario de la lengua española*, the official Spanish dictionary, in 1914. Like *champaña*, it has, at the understandable insistence of the French producers, been disused on labels and as an official description long since, but is still colloquial Spanish for brandy. Nobody, for example, ordering coffee and brandy in a bar, would ask for anything except '*café y coñac*'.

In the early days Spanish brandy was, in fact, made in identical fashion to cognac – which was hardly surprising, as a pioneer like Juan Hernández Rubio, who set up the first concern solely to make brandy, Riva y Rubio y Cia (now owned by Diez-Mérito) in 1882, first studied the production of cognac in the Charente. The spirit was double-distilled in a simple pot still, the 'headings' and 'tailings' being rejected and only the 'heart' or middle fraction of the distillate being retained. Some of the very early stills, like those preserved at González Byass, do not look very different from those of the woodcut illustrations in Brunschwick's famous *Das Buch zu Distillieren* of 1507, but as more and more of the sherry houses, such as Terry, Osborne and Bobadilla, began making brandy, state-of-the-art equipment was bought from France or patterned on French models. Some of these complicated and beautiful old copper stills, like that standing some 30 feet high in the Valdespino bodegas, still survive – though Don Miguel Valdespino tells me that it is almost a century since it was last used. It is revealing that the companies which did *not* engage in making brandy were the British-owned, reflecting the opinion that the native-made brandy could not compare with cognac. Matters have now turned full circle; one of the main objects of the recent purchase of Terry by Harveys of Bristol was to enter into the lucrative market for Spanish brandy.

To begin with the raw brandy was matured along French lines in a single oak cask (as it still is in Catalonia, where it also continues to be made by discontinuous distillation in Charentais-type stills). However, it was inevitable in Jerez, that the producers should begin maturing brandy, like sherry, by the *solera* system, thus endowing the spirit with characteristics very much its own.

The other great difference between French and Spanish brandies is that the great bulk of the Spanish is now made by continuous distillation of spirit, at low strength so as to preserve the volatile flavouring elements or 'congeners'.

MAKING AND AGEING OF JEREZ BRANDY

Distillation of the grape spirit and maturation of Jerez brandy are not now normally carried out in the same establishment. The Palomino grapes grown in the sherry area are too expensive to employ for distillation except in small quantity for very special brandies, and the spirit is produced in distilleries up and down the country and transported to Jerez de la Frontera for elaboration. The largest supplier is the great central area of La Mancha where the prevalent grape is the thick-skinned white Airén, which flourishes on poor soils and withstands extremes of climate. It does not make particularly distinguished table wines, but they have proved very suitable for brandy-making. In 1983 the large co-operatives of the region produced 4·5 million hectolitres of wine for this purpose; other important suppliers were the Extremadura on the Portuguese border with 760,000 hectolitres and the Valencian area with 176,000.

Most of the distilleries are concentrated in Tomelloso, a little town in the dusty heart of the Don Quixote country – but well-known in Spain because its name is writ large on the silver tank cars of the Alcoholera Española, a familiar sight on the railway line south through Córdoba and Seville. Apart from the massive installations of the Alcoholera, various of the large sherry firms operate their own distilleries in

Tomelloso and also in Almendralejo, another hot and dusty wine township in the Extremadura, and in Bolullos del Condado in the province of Huelva west of Jerez, where Domecq have a distillery.

The spirit is distilled in 'continuous' stills, the wine being fed into a tall steam-heated column, resembling the Coffey stills used for making grain whisky, and emerging in a steady stream. Obviously a column of this type is far more economic to operate than a traditional discontinuous pot still, with which operations have to be started anew with each fresh batch. The disadvantage of the continuous process is that if it is operated at high temperature to yield a spirit high in alcohol, few of the congeners or non-alcohols which give bouquet and flavour to a brandy will remain. For this reason, the best of the grape spirit for brandy-making is the *holandas* distilled at low temperature, containing 60–70 per cent of alcohol and rich in the flavour-bearing congeners. Spirit made in *alquitaras* (discontinuous stills of the Charentais type) is even more positive in character, but is made only in small amount for premium brandies.

A Consejo Regulador and a *denominación específica 'Brandy de Jerez'* were established in 1987 (see Chapter 3). The *Reglamento* lays down that only grape spirit may be used in making Jerez brandy and specifically excludes neutral spirit from other sources. It defines the different types of *aguardiente de vino* (or grape spirit) suitable for making Jerez brandy as:

A. *Aguardientes de vino* of low and medium degree.
a. *Aguardiente de vino* of low degree, traditionally known as *holanda de vino*, is grape spirit containing not more than 70° (per cent by volume) of alcohol.
b. *Aguardiente de vino* of medium degree is grape spirit with alcoholic degree of not more than 80°.

B. *Aguardiente de vino* of high degree ('Destilado del vino'). This is obtained by the distillation of wine, or of *aguardiente de vino* of low or medium degree, and its alcohol content is above 80°.

The higher the proportion of the aromatic *holandas*, the better the brandy: fine brandies are made entirely with *holandas* or with spirit from *alquitaras*.

For the best brandies the raw spirit is aged in separate small casks, as in Cognac and Catalonia, until a reduction in alcoholic strength is achieved before transfer to a *solera*. For ordinary brandies, the grape spirit is broken down with distilled water soon after distillation, leaving it with a strength of some 44° of alcohol (brandies lose strength during maturation, and the *Reglamento* stipulates that the final strength must lie between 34° and 45°). If a darker coloured or sweetened brandy is required, small amounts of caramel and syrup are added, and the spirit then begins its 'education' in the oak casks of a *solera*. This is organised in exactly the same way as a sherry *solera*, consisting of *criaderas* and a bottom row of casks, the *solera* proper, from which at intervals brandy is withdrawn for bottling, and consisting of up to fourteen 'scales' in all arranged in tiers of three or four casks. The casks are normally made of American oak and may be new or have been used for sherry, but old brandy casks are not used as over the years the spirit attacks the wood. One of the most impressive buildings in Jerez is the brandy store constructed by Pedro Domecq with diminishing vistas of Moorish-style horse-shoe arches and thousand upon thousand barrels of slowly maturing brandy.

The dynamic ageing of Jerez brandy in a *solera* where it may be moved from cask to cask several times a year affects both the rate of the maturation process and the character of the end product. Because it is more exposed to air than cognac, which is aged statically in a single cask, Jerez brandy is on the way to becoming smooth and drinkable within a year, whereas a young cognac requires at least three. The fractional blending of spirits of different ages also leads to differences in the chain of chemical reactions, involving tannins from the oak, ester reactions and an increase in acids and aldehydes. Another result of maturing brandy in a *solera* is the uniformity of the product. As Richard Ford remarked of sherry, 'The contents of one barrel serve to correct another until the proposed standard aggregate is produced.'

STYLES OF JEREZ BRANDY

There is great variation both in the age and styles of Jerez brandy. The *Reglamento* defines a basic three types:

> *Brandy de Jerez. Solera.* This is a brandy elaborated with *aguardientes de vino* matured for more than six months. Its content of non-alcohols, i.e. the total of volatile acids, aldehydes, esters and higher alcohols, must be more than 200 mg per 100 cc absolute alcohol.

> *Brandy de Jerez. Solera Reserva.* Brandy elaborated with *aguardiente de*

vino matured for more than a year. The content of non-alcohols must be more than 250 mg per 100 cc absolute alcohol.

Brandy de Jerez. Gran Reserva. Brandy elaborated with *aguardiente de vino* and matured for more than three years. The content of non-alcohols must be more than 300 mg per 100 cc absolute alcohol.

These are minimum requirements and the older brandies are matured for much longer.

The biggest-selling of the cheaper brandies are 'Soberano' from González Byass, 'Veterano' from Osborne and Terry's 'Centenario'. Perhaps because until very recently González Byass was partly English-owned,the driest and lightest in colour of these is 'Soberano'. The other two are somewhat darker in colour and a little sweetened to the Spanish taste. 'Veterano', proclaimed by the silhouetted cutouts of bulls along every main road in Spain, gains part of its fruity flavour by enrichment with macerated plums and nuts. 'Fundador' from Pedro Domecq has lost ground in the domestic market, if not abroad; for foreign tastes it remains one of the best of the less expensive brandies, containing as it does some fifty per cent of *holandas*, so giving it more of a genuine grapey flavour than some of its competitors made with a higher proportion of higher strength *aguardiente* with less of the flavouring elements. Other good brandies in this price bracket, dry in style and with a character derived from *holandas* and oak rather than additives, are Bobadilla's '103' and 'Felipe II' from Agustín Blázquez.

The consumption of brandy in Spain by far outruns that of sherry, and over the last decade there has been a big swing towards the medium-priced brandies (of which Nicholas Faith reports that current sales of over two million cases are more than twice the total production of *armagnac*). Here, the dark, smooth and fragrant 'Magno' from Osborne, slightly sweetened but not aggressively so, is the clear brand leader. As in the other categories, there is a large choice. If you prefer a drier brandy, you should ask, for example, for the Bobadilla 'Gran Capitán' or González Byass 'Insuperable'.

The market for *gran reservas* is much more restricted, though they embrace the most characterful and sophisticated of Jerez brandies. Again, the best-known are poles apart in style. At one extreme is González Byass's 'Lepanto', sold in a glass decanter. It is made with pure *holandas*, some of it distilled from Palomino wine, and appeals to connoisseurs of cognac. Pale golden in colour, it is dry, light and delicate, with a touch of vanilla and elegant nose bespeaking long age in oak. At the other end of the scale is 'Independencia' from Osborne, rich, mellow, dark and sweet, though its running mate 'Conde de Osborne', presented in a white ceramic container, designed by Salvador Dalí and apparently slumping under the weight of years, is light, unsweetened and spirituous. The 'Marqués de Domecq' is a fine example of the best of Jerez brandy, full and round, without artificial sweetening, and owing its character to a grape spirit high in non-alcohols and long ageing in the oak of a *solera*.

The other houses have their fine brandies, such as the 'Renacimiento' from Garvey, 'Gran Duque de Alba' from Diez-Mérito and the '103 Etiqueta Negra' from Bobadilla, but one that deserves a special note is 'Cardenal Mendoza', which has started something of a cult. It was first produced in 1887 by the small firm of Sánchez Romate, which remains in private hands. Production is limited to 50,000 cases, most of which go abroad. The spirit is double-distilled and aged in the same oak cask for some years before passing to the *solera*, of which the butts have previously been used for sherry, thus giving this deep, oaky and intense brandy the added complexity of a hint of *oloroso*.

PONCHE

Apart from tonic or medicated wines, such as 'Jerez-Quina', containing quinine extract and administered to children in Spain when they are off colour, Jerez makes an excellent liqueur in the form of *ponche*. This was first produced by the family firm of José de Soto, whose brand is still one of the best and whose handsome silvered bottle carries a label embodying a gaggle of gold medals from international exhibitions of the 1890s and early 1900s held in London, Brussels, Bordeaux, Paris and Madrid. *Ponche* is now made and marketed by a number of firms, and the composition varies somewhat but always includes brandy and orange extract.

The biggest selling brand, advertised by posters of a bosomy and sultry redhead, is made by Luís Caballero, who dispose of an annual 1·2 million cases in the domestic market. Of 30° strength, they make it with a young brandy, adding freshly-made orange concentrate, together with sugar, almond extract and vanilla. In other versions a little sherry is also used. Another excellent brand is the 'Ponche Español' of J. Ruiz, the first of the firms to be absorbed by RUMASA.

Ponche is not a 'sticky' liqueur nor unduly sweet, but light and fluid, with a very fresh orange taste, the faintest hint of coffee or liquorice and a bitter-sweet finish. It is an excellent digestif.

CHAPTER 8

The Cuisine of the Sherry Region

BY MAITE MANJÓN

31 *In Spain it is customary to buy fresh vegetables, fish and meat from market stalls*

The sherry region is rich in culinary resources, growing vegetables and fruit in abundance and drawing on the Bay of Cádiz for a great variety of fish and shellfish. Lying at the southern tip of the Peninsula within shouting distance of Gibraltar and the African coast, it is also one through which successive waves of foreign invaders have entered Spain.

The Carthaginians introduced the *garbanzo* or chick-pea, now a staple of the rich stews or *cocidos* cooked up and down Spain; the Romans reorganised the whole system of agriculture, extending the cultivation of vines and cereals and introducing garlic and olive oil; but it was the Moors, who invaded Spain in 711 and remained in occupation of Andalucía for the next three hundred years, who most firmly left their mark on its cuisine. Not only did they introduce spices such as saffron, nutmeg and black pepper, but also sugar cane, bitter oranges, lemons and almonds. Certain individual dishes, such as *gazpacho*, the famous cold soup, can definitely be attributed to the Moors, and they are also responsible for the great variety of sweetmeats made from egg-yolks and almonds – a tradition maintained by the nuns after the Reconquest and in later days given a fillip by the need of the sherry bodegas to dispose of the egg yolks surplus to the fining of the wines by the whites.

It was not only the ancients and the Moors who introduced novel culinary ingredients to the region. Later on, during the fifteenth and sixteenth centuries, the Conquistadores brought back such exotics as potatoes, peppers, tomatoes and chocolate, until then unknown in Europe. It was through Cádiz and Seville, then an important port, as the River Guadalquivir was navigable to the small sailing ships of the time, that these products were first brought to Spain, so that Andalucía was the first to benefit. Sherry itself is, of course, an important ingredient in cooking, which I shall touch on later.

REGIONAL DISHES

Perhaps the best way to describe the regional cuisine is in the context of a typical meal such as might be served in Cádiz, Jerez de la Frontera or Sanlúcar de Barrameda.

Tapas

All meals in Jerez begin with chilled *fino* as an apéritif, served with *tapas*. *Tapas* are becoming so fashionable abroad in elaborate versions and whole books have been written about dishes that better suit the dinner table, that it is easy to forget that the word originally meant a 'cover' and that its use as an appetiser most probably sprang from the pleasant custom in Andalucían bars of covering the glass with a saucer containing a few almonds, olives, prawns or chunky home-made potato crisps, served with the compliments of the house.

Nowadays, *tapas* are no longer free and most bars have a spread along the counter. They range from the cold, such as *ensaladilla rusa* (Russian salad), *chorizos* (cured paprika sausages), *jamón Jabugo* or *pata negra* (the local and best variety of *jamón serrano*, akin to Parma or Bayonne ham), asparagus, *tortilla de patatas* (the thick Spanish omelette made with potatoes and onions) and marinated mussels or clams, to hot dishes. These embrace small (or not so small) portions, often served in earthenware *cazuelas*, of dishes such as *calamares en su tinta* (squid cooked in its ink), grilled sardines and *boquerones* (fresh anchovies), *caracoles* (snails), *gambas al pilpil* (prawns in garlic sauce), *tortillitas de camarones* (crisp fritters, made with a batter and tiny shrimps and fried in oil) or *huevos a la flamenca* (a dish served straight from the fire in a small *cazuela* and made by breaking eggs over thin rounds of *chorizo* and garnishing it with prawns).

The Bay of Cádiz provides varieties of fish and shellfish not normally found in Mediterranean waters, and some of the *tapas* and starters entirely individual to the region are: *boquerones de la Isla*, fresh anchovies marinated in vinegar, parsley and onion; *cazón*, baby shark, marinated with paprika and vinegar; *barbujitos*, small fresh anchovies, fried; *acedías fritas*, fried baby sole; *cañaíllas de la Isla*, the sea-snail from which the ancients extracted Tyrian purple, which is lightly boiled and served cold; *coquinas al ajillo*, cockles in garlic sauce; and *puntillitas*, minute squid, known in other parts of Spain as *chipirones*, which are dipped in light batter and fried in olive oil.

Soups and starters

Progressing to the meal proper, a favourite starter in Jerez, especially in hot weather, is melon. Small, sweet and full of juice, they are often served with a few slices of *jamón Jabugo* (see above). Another hot weather favourite is the famous Moorish-inspired cold soup, *gazpacho*. The best-known version contains chopped or puréed tomatoes, cucumber and green peppers, together with a little olive oil, garlic and vinegar – lemon juice is kinder if you are drinking wine. Breadcrumbs may either be used in making it or served on the side. Another variation of *gazpacho* is *ajo blanco con uvas de Málaga*, made with ground almonds and whole fresh grapes.

During the short winter, *gazpacho* is also served hot. Other soups include *sopa de pescado gaditano*, a rich fish soup akin to *bouillabaisse*; the delicious *sopa al cuarto de hora*, made with the local *ostiones* or Portuguese oysters, diced ham and hard-boiled eggs and so-called because it is cooked for quarter-of-an-hour; *sopa A B*, named after the González Byass *amontillado* it contains; and, of course, the consommés, into which it is usual to pour a small glass of *fino* at the table.

Fish

The fish from the Bay of Cádiz is legendary for its quality and freshness. It is worth paying a visit to the great open markets in Cádiz or Jerez to see it in all its variety – tuna; sardines; fresh anchovies; *chocos* (cuttlefish); swordfish; the gleaming scabbard fish; the ugly but delicious *'perros'* and *'gatos'* ('dogs' and 'cats'); the even uglier *rascasio*, essential for *bouillabaisse*; the carnivorous and gamy *urta*; and the shad, such a favourite of the Moors, which swims up the rivers in spring; together with piles of shellfish of every sort and variety. Fish restaurants like Bigote in Sanlúcar de Barrameda and El Faro in Cádiz buy straight from the fishermen, some of whom catch it with rod and line.

A traditional method of catching fish along the Atlantic coasts of Cádiz and Huelva is to allow it to swim into *caños* or salt pools, which are then dammed up. The salinity of the water increases because of evaporation, giving the fish an exceptionally good flavour, and when they have grown and multiplied the pool is emptied and the owner and his friends gather to scoop them out.

On gastronomic maps of Spain, Andalucía is often labelled the *Zona de los fritos* or 'region of fried food', and an institution in Cádiz is the *freidurías*, where fried fish may be eaten on the premises or bought to take away, and of which the famous revivalist of traditional Spanish cooking, 'Dr Thebussem', once wrote;

> Because of the special and secret method of cutting the fish and the temperature of the oil, the aroma rising from the sole, mullet, whiting, sardines and other fish cooking in the steaming olive oil is an invitation to eat; and few suppers are more agreeable than this fried fish, washed down by half-a-dozen glasses of aromatic manzanilla.

One of the most famous of the fish dishes from the Cádiz region is the *pareja* or fry of mixed fish. Also known as *fritura gaditana*, it takes its name from a dish cooked by the fishermen while at sea in their boats, and contains a variety of small fish, such as sardines, fresh anchovies, small squid and *acedías* (small soles), fried crisp golden-brown in sizzling olive oil. An unusual method of cooking *dorada* (gilthead) is to bake it in a thick paste of sea salt, which is removed by the waiter at the table, leaving the fish juicy and full of flavour. The ribbon-like and gleaming silver *paire* (scabbard fish) is cut diagonally into steaks and cooked under the grill and is, to my mind, a lot more succulent and appetising than *pez espada* (swordfish) with which it is often confused – just to make matters easy, the Portuguese call scabbard fish *pez espada*!

A dish which you will often see on menus is *urta a la roteña*. *Urta* (*dentex dentex*) is another ugly-looking customer, for which there is no name in English and suggestions, which I have seen in American books, that it can be replaced by porgy are absurd. It is fished only in the waters off Rota in the Bay of Cádiz and feeds on small shellfish, which gives it an almost shellfish-like flavour itself. It is cooked in a rich sauce made with green peppers, tomatoes and onions with *fino* sherry.

I have left the shellfish to the last, but the magnificent *gambas* (prawns), *cigalas* (sea crayfish), *langostinos* (Dublin Bay prawns), *langosta* (spiny lobster) or *bogavante* (lobster), sometimes displayed in a refrigerated showcase at the entrance of the restaurant, may well tempt you to look no further. They are usually eaten cold with mayonnaise and washed down with cold *fino*.

Meat and game

The Jerezanos eat more fish than meat, but there is game in plenty. The *bodegueros* are often as keen on shooting as on polo (many of them, indeed, come regularly to Scotland for the deer stalking) and regularly hunt *caza mayor* (deer, roebuck and wild boar) in the mountainous Sierra de Cádiz between Jerez and the Sierra de Ronda. *Corzo*, a small roe deer from here, is tenderer than the venison from a larger animal, and is usually marinated for three or four days in *oloroso* and sherry vinegar before roasting or stewing.

What you are more likely to encounter in a restaurant is *caza menor*, the fruits of the rough shooting in the fields which goes on all over Spain on Sundays. It includes rabbits, hares, woodcock, pheasant, partridge and pigeon, prepared in such novel ways as *perdices a la torera* ('bullfighter's partridge'), which are garnished with bacon, anchovies, green peppers and tomatoes.

The Jerezanos also have their own ways with beef, notably *bistec salteado al Jerez* (steak sautéed with sherry), but perhaps best-known of Andalucan meat dishes is *rabo de toro a la andaluza* (oxtail Andalucían style), cooked with onions, carrots and herbs, and served with a sauce made with *fino* or *oloroso* sherry. Another dish entirely typical of the region is *riñones al Jerez* (kidneys with sherry), for which small kidneys are sliced, sautéed in hot olive oil, and then cooked slowly with a freshly-made tomato sauce and dry sherry.

Postres

This is a useful Spanish word, translatable as 'afters' – anything that follows the main course. There is not a wide choice of sweets in

Andalucía or Spain generally. The most common is *flan* or baked cream caramel, which is made very well. Running it close in Andalucía is *tocino de cielo*, *not* 'little pigs from the sky' as I have seen it translated in Anglo-Saxon accounts of Spanish cooking but a sweet made from eggs and vanilla-scented sugar. What are really delicious are the ice creams made with *turrón* (Spanish nougat) and the *helado de pasas al Pedro Ximénez*. This is an ice cream made with raisins and the intensely sweet and raisiny Pedro Ximénez sherry, over which it is customary to pour a further libation of Pedro Ximénez and which is made to perfection in Bigote's restaurant in Sanlúcar de Barrameda. Many restaurants also sport a trolley with a selection of *tartas heladas*, iced tarts and cakes with glazed fruits.

In place of a sweet, the Spanish often finish a meal with fresh fruit. The small melons are as delicious after a meal as before, and the local strawberries, of which there are two crops, are available much earlier than in Britain. A small glass of a good sweet *oloroso*, poured over them, is the ideal accompaniment. Fresh figs, so expensive here, are abundant, but usually not available in elegant restaurants as being considered too commonplace. Incidentally, should you tire of sherry, wonderfully fresh orange juice is available all year round.

If you want cheese you must ask for it and also for bread, as the Spanish eat it on its own with a knife and fork or with *membrillo*, a stiff quince paste – an addiction with Pedro de Luna, the last of the Antipopes, whose Roman enemies unsuccessfully tried to kill him by dosing it with arsenic during his exile in Peñíscola. A local cheese worth asking for is the *Queso de Cádiz*, a firm white cheese with pleasant, mellow flavour, made from goat's milk and pressed in esparto baskets, so that the golden rind bears the pattern of the mould. It is more likely that you will be served with *Queso Manchego* from La Mancha, which is to Spain what Cheddar is to England. Also made from goat's milk, it acquires character and bite when matured in olive oil.

Lastly, there is a profusion of small cakes and sweetmeats. Usually made from egg yolks and almonds, these are a legacy of the Moors, but after the Reconquest the nuns took to making them in their convents and selling them to swell the religious coffers. The tradition was maintained when the bodegas needed an outlet for the egg yolks left on their hands after the whites had been separated and used for clarifying their wines. Another confection typical of the region are the *polvorones*, a powdery sweetmeat made with ground almonds and icing sugar. In Estepa, on the way from Córdoba to Málaga, the manufactories line the main road and the air is redolent with the fragrance of toasted almonds. They are wrapped in twists of paper and are often eaten in Andalucía with a glass of sherry as 'elevenses' or in the afternoon.

COOKING WITH SHERRY

Few people interested in cooking can be unaware of the culinary uses of sherry. At the simplest level a dash of *fino* added to a consommé or of *amontillado* to more robust soups improves even the canned variety out of all recognition.

The first point which I should like to make is that it is profitless to use cheap sherry-type wine from other countries in place of genuine sherry. The results are much the same as when one opens a bottle of red wine, decides that it is too rough or too acid to drink, and adds it to a stew – thus ruining it. With the price of meat and fish as they are, a little decent sherry is no great extravagance.

The most widespread use of sherry is in making sauces; for the more delicate use *fino*. Dry *olorosos* do a great deal for meats and can with advantage be added in the final stages of making gravy. Sweet *oloroso* or cream sherry is the making of fruit salads and trifles; it can also be used in making sweet pastries.

These are only the most general suggestions, and those interested in the sophisticated uses of sherry in cooking and in individual dishes should obtain a copy of *Cooking with sherry* (Espasa-Calpe, Madrid, 1983) by Lalo Grosso de Macpherson, who enjoys the titles both of *Cocinera de Jerez* ('Cook of Jerez') and *Cocinera del Rey* ('Royal Cook'). In it, you will find scores of recipes illustrating the employment of the different styles of sherry in sauces, marinades and soups, in cooking vegetables, fish, game and meat and in making sweets. Her recipes are *not* purely Spanish; the original Spanish version is, indeed, entitled *El vino de Jerez en la cocina universal*.

RESTAURANTS
(For hotels see Chapter 1)

Cádiz
*El Faro***
San Felix, 15; tel. 21 10 68.
A sophisticated restaurant serving a wide variety of fish from the Bay of Cádiz. Gonzalo de Córdoba buys both from the fishermen and the

market and you will find many local specialities, such as *acedías* (baby sole), *cañaíllas de la Isla* (sea snails), and *pijotas* (tiny fish fried like whitebait). Specialities include the crisp-fried shrimp fritters, *dorada a la sal* (gilthead baked in a paste of sea salt) and *urta* (see page 107).

Mesón del Duque*
Paseo Marítimo, 12; tel. 28 10 87.
Fish from the Bay of Cádiz and well-cooked Andalucian dishes. Rioja and wines from the region.

Jerez de la Frontera
El Bosque*
Avenida Alvaro Domecq, 26; tel. 33 33 33.
Well-known Jerez restaurant situated in a park with charming ambience. International and regional cuisine; good wine list.

Gaitán*
Gaitán, 3; tel. 34 58 59.
This restaurant built up a reputation for Andalucían and Basque food under Antonio Orihuela, but has changed hands and been enlarged. Though still one of Jerez's leading restaurants, it has not quite the panache that it used to have.

La Mesa Redonda**
Calle Urbis, off Avenida Alvaro Domecq; tel. 34 00 59.
Newly opened by José Antonio Valdespino and Margarita López de Carrizosa, former proprietors of the much lamented Hotel Los Cisnes, this is a charming and most individual little restaurant where one may browse among a small library of books on gastronomy over a glass of *fino* or dine outside at a table on the quiet, shaded pavement in the warmth of a summer's evening. Sr. Valdespino is personally in charge of the kitchen and the short but well chosen menu varies according to what is best and freshest in the market. The cold gazpacho is the best I know and other specialities include admirably fresh *vieiras* (scallops) and grilled salmon in season.

Tendido*
Circo, 10; tel. 34 48 35.
Large, bustling and cheerful, and centrally located opposite the bullring, this is one of Jerez's most popular restaurants, serving a range of local dishes.

Puerto de Santa María
*La Goleta***
Crtra de Rota, 1·5 km; tel. 85 42 32
Just outside and overlooking the town, the restaurant is modern and comfortable with an attractive terrace. Sophisticated cooking and first-rate seafood.

*Guadalete**
Facing the river of the same name and the quays, this is a crowded and thoroughly typical place (the local football team was eating outside at a trestle table when I was last there), serving such favourites as *rape en salsa verde* (angler fish in green sauce), *chipirones en tinta* (small squid in their ink) and *lubina en horno* (baked sea bass).

Sanlúcar de Barrameda
*Bigote***
Bajo de Guía, s/n; tel. 36 26 96.
Bigote started very humbly as a fisherman's tavern, its proprietor being nicknamed 'bigote' because of his moustache. His sons Paco and Fernando 'Bigote' (nobody seems to know their real surname) have turned it into one of the best places to eat fish and seafood in Andalucía. There is no menu; they simply tell their guests what is fresh from the Bay of Cádiz and available at the time of their visit. Nevertheless some of their dishes, such as the *raya a la naranja agria* (angler fish with bitter orange) are a legend. They refuse to extend the restaurant, which cannot serve more than 150 lunches, and to make sure of a table it is often necessary to telephone several days in advance.

Seville
There is no shortage of sophisticated restaurants in Seville, such as *Paco Ramos*, *San Marco* and *Rincón de Curro*, or *Albahaca*, charmingly situated in the Barrio de Santa Cruz, the old Jewish quarter. The adventurous may, however, prefer to chance an arm in the *tapa* places of Triana; if so it is advisable to get hold of a copy of *Guía del tapeo en Triana* (published by the Municipality of Seville and obtainable from the Tourist Office), which lists scores of such establishments, together with their specialities and a useful map.

THE BODEGAS

AND THEIR WINES

This is an almost complete descriptive listing of the Bodegas de Crianza y Expedición, *i.e. those which mature and ship sherry. A few other firms, which have been taken over but whose labels still exist, are also included. Also listed are some of the leading* almacenistas *or 'stockholders', whose wines are available abroad, and the eight co-operatives in the sherry region.*

Where necessary, the exact location of a bodega is given after the address, by its distance from Madrid on the road, for example: 'Crtra Madrid–Cadiz, km 641·7, Jerez.

Jerez de la Frontera

Abad, S.A., Tomás
P.O. Box 337, Muro de la Merced, 28, 1104 Jerez.
This small firm was founded in 1870 by Don Cecilio Abad y Pérez from Santander. Its bodegas, housing some 2,000 butts, stand on a hill overlooking the harbour of Puerto de Santa María. The firm markets a wide range of sherries under the label of Tomás Abad, but is now a subsidiary of EMILIO LUSTAU.

Almacenistas
It is difficult to find an exact translation of the word *almacenista*; the nearest is, perhaps, 'stockholder'. They are in practice small concerns which mature *mosto* from their own vineyards or bought from individual growers. The *almacenistas* are registered under Category D of the Consejo Regulador as *bodegas de crianza*, but may not, unless further registered under Category C as a *bodega de crianza y expedición*, export sherry, nor do they sell directly to the public. Their function is to acquire and mature parcels of fine sherry, often from single vineyards, which they sell to the large shippers for improving their commercial sherries. Some of their wines, like the superb old *olorosos* which I have tasted in the bodegas of the Viuda de Carmen Borrego,

32 Patio in the Palacio Domecq

are so intense and concentrated in flavour that they are for nosing and tasting rather than drinking – or, of course, for blending. The *almacenistas* are therefore suppliers and guardians (most are personally dedicated to their vocation) of single vineyard, unblended sherries. There are at present thirty-two of them in Jerez de la Frontera, two in Puerto de Santa María and thirty in Sanlúcar de Barrameda.

The firm that has specialised in bottling and shipping fine *almacenista* wines is EMILIO LUSTAU, which lists its suppliers as:

Aranda, Doña Pilar (*Jerez*)
Benítez Girón, Doña Rosario (*Jerez*)
Bohorquez Vegazo, Don José (*Jerez*)
Carbajo Gutiérrez, Don Miguel (*Sanlúcar de Barrameda*)
Carrasco, Don Fernando (*Jerez*)
Cayetano del Pino y Cia. (*Jerez*)
Colosia Molleda, Doña Ma. Loreto (*Puerto de Sta María*)
Cuevas Jurado, Don Manuel (*Sanlúcar de Barrameda*)
Farfante Rodríguez, Doña Ma. Rosario (*Jerez*)
Fontádez Florido, Don Miguel (*Jerez*)
García Angulo, Don José Ramón (*Jerez*)
García Jarana, Bodegas (*Jerez*)
González y Cia, Bodegas (*Puerto de Sta María*)
Guerrero Ortega, Don José María (*Jerez*)
Herederos de Argueso (*Sanlúcar de Barrameda*)
Hidalgo Colón, Don Manuel J. (*Sanlúcar de Barrameda*)
Hijos de Julio Coveñas (*Jerez*)
Lorente Piaget, Don Alberto (*Jerez*)
Rodríguez y Otaolaurruchi (*Sanlúcar de Barrameda*)
San Cayetano, Bodegas (*Sanlúcar de Barrameda*)
Sucesores de Diego García Pérez y Victor (*Jerez*)
Viuda de Antonio Borrego (*Jerez*)

A figure, such as 1/17 or 1/40, found on the labels of some *almacenista* wines refers to the number of butts in the *solera* from which the wine has been drawn, i.e. seventeen or forty butts in these instances. The smaller the number, the rarer is the wine.

Bertola, S.A.

Box 140, Crtra N–IV, s/n., Jerez.

Bertola was formed in 1911, when C.N. Kopke & Co Ltd, perhaps the oldest of the port firms, decided to enter the sherry trade and set up a Spanish subsidiary, Kopke Bertola y Cia Ltda. The firm subsequently became a subsidiary of DIEZ HERMANOS and was later sold to RUMASA and incorporated in BODEGAS INTERNACIONALES. On the collapse of RUMASA, it was taken over as part of Bodegas Internacionales by the new Sherry and Rioja tycoon, Marcos Eguizábal.

There are still 600 hectares of vineyards in Jerez Superior in the name of Bertola, but the wines are made and matured in the vast new bodegas of BODEGAS INTERNACIONALES. They include a crisp *manzanilla*; a light, dry *fino* and a round, nutty *amontillado*; but the wine for which the firm is best known is its luscious 'Bertola Cream', especially popular in Scotland.

Blázquez, S.A., Hijos de Agustín
P.O. Box 540, Crtra Jerez–Algeciras.
The original Agustín Blázquez was from Cádiz, where he owned bodegas. In 1857 he transferred to Jerez, taking over the old *soleras* of his grandfather, Francisco Paul, and establishing Hijos de Agustín Blázquez. He was soon in possession of some 11,000 butts and exporting his *fino* 'Carta Blanca' and old *amontillado* 'Carta Oro' in large amount to Cuba.

The firm was taken over by PEDRO DOMECQ in 1973, but operates independently with separate premises in Jerez and Puerto de Sta María. 'Carta Blanca' remains one of the best, driest and roundest of *finos* and 'Carta Oro' a fine old *amontillado*. Other specialities are the 'Carta Roja' *oloroso* and 'Capuchino' *palo cortado*. More recently the firm has introduced a range of 'Balfour' wines. It also makes the popular 'Felipe II' brandy and a premium quality 'Toisón de Oro'.

Exports of sherry and brandy to Holland, Italy and the United States amount to more than a million cases annually.

Bobadilla y Cia
P.O. Box 217, Crtra Circunvalación, s/n., Jerez.
BOBADILLA is the name under which are marketed the sherries and brandies of BODEGAS MANUEL FERNÁNDEZ, S.A. The firm was founded in 1879 by Don Manuel Fernández de Bobadilla y Martínez, whose original bodega was within the monastery of Los Padres Mercedarios. The firm now operates from a new bodega just outside Jerez on the road to Cádiz and owns three vineyards, totalling 150 hectares in all. The descendants of Don Manuel are still actively involved.

Bobadilla is best known in Spain for its big-selling '103' brandy (there is also an oaky and more mature 'Gran Capitán') but also makes some good sherries, including a 'Victoria' *fino*, 'Capitán' *oloroso*, 'Alcázar' *amontillado* and 'La Merced' cream.

Bustamente, S.L., José
San Francisco Javier, 3, Jerez.
One of the smaller firms making a complete range of sherries and brandies, of which the best known are 'Betis' *fino*, 'Paso Doble' *amontillado* and 'Fragata' medium *oloroso*.

Cayetano del Pino y Cia, S.L.
Cardenal Herrero, 6, Jerez.
This firm is both a shipper and *almacenista* (see page 115), whose fine old sherries are available through EMILIO LUSTAU. Its *palo cortado* is a splendid wine with a nutty, smoky *amontillado* nose, smooth and intense and finishing like an *oloroso*.

Co-operatives
There are eight co-operative wineries in the sherry region, which vinify the grapes for their *socios* – the owners of small-to-medium-sized vineyards, of whom there are 4,500. The must is then sold to the private firms to be matured in their *criaderas* and *soleras*. The Cooperativa Virgen de la Caridad in Sanlúcar de Barrameda has its own *soleras* and bottles and sells sherry under its own label – see under C.A.Y.D.S.A. (Sanlúcar de Barrameda).

The other co-operatives, of which Nuestra Señora de las Angustias in Jerez is the most important, are:

Cooperativa Católica-Agrícola,
Avenida de Regla, 15, Chipiona.
Cooperativa del Campo Covisán,
Calle González Hontoria, 6, Sanlúcar de Barrameda.
Cooperativa del Campo San Juan Bautista,
Calle Santísma Trinidad, 16, Chiclana de la Frontera.
Cooperativa Sindical Agrícola Virgen de Palomares,
Avenida de Sevilla, s/n, Trebujena.
Cooperativa Vinícola Jerezana Nuestra Señora de las Angustias,
P.O. Box 253, Crtra de Circunvalación, s/n, Jerez.
Cooperativa Vitivinícola Albarizas,
Crtra de Trebujena, s/n, Trebbujena.
Pago de Miraflores Sociedad Cooperativa Ltda,
Calle Borregueros, 24, Sanlúcar de Barrameda.

Croft Jerez, S.A.

P.O. Box 414, Crtra Circunvalación, km. 636·3, Jerez.

Although Croft is one of the newest and most enterprising of the
sherry houses, its history goes back to 1678, when John Croft, of an
old Yorkshire family, helped to found the port company of Tilden,
Thompson and Croft. In 1769 the firm was rechristened Croft & Co.
and later developed ties with W.A. Gilbey, the famous shippers of both
port and sherry, who finally bought it in 1911. Gilbey's marketed
sherry on a large scale, but their *soleras* were managed by GONZALEZ
BYASS. (The Gilbey and González families are also related by
marriage.) In 1962 Gilbey's merged with two other companies to form
International Vintners & Distillers, and in 1970 it was decided to
reorganise the sherry arm of the combine with the entry of Croft into
the sherry business.

The operation was based on the old Gilbey *soleras* and wines
acquired from other bodegas of standing, and with the participation of
the noted firm of DIEZ HERMANOS, which at one time had a large
holding in the company, but pulled out in 1977.

In 1979 designs were commissioned for a huge new complex of
buildings from the architect Vicente Masaveu. The distinguished
restorer of such buildings as the Monastery of Guadalupe, he designed
the handsome Rancho Croft in traditional style – but with provision for
the most advanced technology – and the buildings are entirely in
keeping with the surroundings. They house two of the most modern
continuous presses in Jerez (see page 50), allowing for some 70 per
cent of free-run must (of which some 90 per cent develops as *fino*),
and later, by increasing the pressure, for a higher rate of extraction and
musts used for *olorosos* and distillation; serried rows of stainless steel
fermentation tanks; and the latest in filtration and refrigeration
machinery. The adjoining five bodegas, with white walls and tiled
roofs, house some 50,000 butts.

So well-planned is the new complex that, although Croft is now the
second largest exporter to the U.K. and responsible for 10 per cent of
sherry exports world-wide, the plant is run by a work force of only 60,
– one of the reasons why, while other bodegas have suffered from the
current depression, the story here has been of continuous
expansion.

The company has 370 hectares of vineyards and another 350 which
it cannot at the moment plant because of current restrictions on the
area under plantation, and like the other big concerns buys in grapes
from independent growers.

Its *soleras* are of two kinds: those long ago laid down by the Gilbeys,

such as Doña Gracia, Picazo and Los Graciosos, and others like
Delicado or Odette y Correa dating from the Croft era. By Los
Graciosos there hangs an amusing tale. Towards the end of the last
century some members of the Gilbey family on a visit to the *soleras*
brought with them their young twin sons, dressed exactly alike. The
capataz exclaimed '*Que gracioso!*' ('How funny!'), continuing in Spanish,
'This wine is making me see the child double.' The father, taking the
word '*gracioso*' for a compliment, asked that the *solera* should be named
in honour of his children, and it has been known as 'Los Graciosos'
ever since.

33 Unloading grapes at Croft's bodega for crushing

Apart from the efficiency of the operation another reason for Croft's
success has been a marketing philosophy based on the premise that
one should find out what the consumer wants, and then set about
making and selling it. So it was that they developed the first of the
pale cream sherries, 'Croft Original', made by sweetening a blend of
fino and pale *amontillado* with a concentrated must decolourised with
activated charcoal, thus obtaining the combination of lightness and
sweetness that has proved so immensely popular in the mass market.
'Croft Original' is now the No. 2 seller in the U.K. and also sells
extremely well in the United States and the other 70 odd countries to
which Croft exports its wines.

'Croft Particular' is along the same lines, pale in colour, round and
smooth, but medium to dry. The other Croft sherries are traditional in
style. the 'Delicado' *fino* is light, dry and elegant with a fresh *flor* nose;
the 'Classic' *amontillado* has a good nutty nose and is full, oaky and
semi-dry; the *palo cortado* is a good example of this less common style,
intense in nose, full-bodied and dry; the old *oloroso* is from a 140-year-
old *solera*, bone-dry, full of flavour, with deep, fragrant nose and long,
long finish.

Diestro, S.A.

P.O. Box 300, Crtra Madrid–Cádiz, km 641·7, Jerez.
This old firm, founded in 1798, was taken over by RUMASA and
incorporated in BODEGAS INTERNACIONALES, now under new
ownership. Its leading brands, sold mainly in Spain, are 'Fino Jardín'
and the quinine-flavoured 'Quina San Ramón'.

Diez-Mérito, S.A.

P.O. Box 7, Crtra Madrid–Cádiz, km 641·7, Jerez.
The company was founded as Diez Hermanos in France, when in 1876
Salvador Diez Pérez de Muñoz began selling sherries in Bayonne
supplied to him by his father in Jerez. Soon afterwards his younger

brothers started a similar business in Marseille and joined forces in buying their own bodega in Jerez. The firm expanded steadily but unostentatiously by selling wine for bottling abroad by the purchaser. Meanwhile the family embarked on the acquisition of a series of small bodegas, beginning with that of José de Fuentes Parilla, dating from 1864 and the first concern in Jerez to ship in bottle rather than butt. In 1924 they started business in Oporto as port shippers; for a time they had a stake in Bertola and also Croft, and later bought the

important firm of the Marqués de Mérito, founded in the mid-nineteenth century by another great Jerez family, the López de Carrizosa. At that point the name was changed to Diez-Mérito. Lorenzo Diez Lacave, who then headed the firm, was also responsible for planting extensive new vineyards and building a new vinification and bottling plant, one of the most modern in Jerez, on the outskirts of the town.

A company so obviously successful was inevitably a target for RUMASA and was one of its last acquisitions. After the collapse of José María Ruíz-Mateos's empire, Diez-Mérito, like the giant BODEGAS INTERNACIONALES, was bought by Don Marcos Eguizábal in 1985, but operates as a separate entity. Ironically enough, it has in its turn taken over Zoilo Ruíz-Mateos S.A. once the flagship of the RUMASA sherry group, and inherited the *soleras* not only of the magnificent 'Don Zoilo' sherries but of the famous 'Gran Duque de Alba' brandy.

As a result of this and its earlier acquisitions, Diez-Mérito has seven vineyards in the Jerez Superior region; five cellars and their *soleras* in Jerez, and the Bodega Arboledilla in Sanlúcar; and the large fermentation, stabilisation and bottling plant just outside Jerez. One of the Jerez bodegas is at La Atalaya, former RUMASA headquarters, but the mansion itself, originally the property of the Vergara family, which served as the head office of the group and housed a magnificent collection of antique clocks and watches, is now (with the collection still intact) the municipal museum.

Diez-Mérito markets a very wide range of high quality sherries under its own and the labels of the different firms it has absorbed over the years. Best known of the wines from Diez Hermanos are the 'Fino Imperial', in fact a fine old *fino-amontillado* from a *solera* laid down in 1793, and the magnificent 'Oloroso Victoria Regina', dry, of dark mahogany colour and intense flavour, from a *solera* started in 1906. Whatever the criticism of the cheaper RUMASA sherries, 'Don Zoilo', named in honour of Don Zoilo Ruíz-Mateos Camacho, who started the family business in a small way in Jerez, was always of superb quality and sold at a premium, and remains so. The range extends to *fino*, *manzanilla*, *amontillado*, medium, *oloroso*, cream, pale cream, Moscatel and Pedro Jimenez, of which the best-known is the *fino*, from a *solera* of 23 *criaderas*, with the smoothness, depth and intensity of a wine with long barrel age under *flor*. Another series of sherries is bottled under the Mérito label; and there is a Mérito rum and brandy, and a Diez-Mérito gin. The group's products are sold internationally, leading markets being the U.K., West Germany, Holland, the United States and Latin America.

Domecq, S.A., Pedro

P.O. Box 80, San Ildefonso, 3, Jerez.

The Domecq family is one of the oldest from Béarn in the Basses-Pyrénées, and it was their privilege from the time of Louis XIV to present each French monarch with a pair of white gloves in token of fealty – hence the motto of the family, 'Domecq Oblige' and their coat of arms featuring a pair of white gloves and a drawn sword on an azure field.

It was, however, only in 1816, eighty-six years after it had been established, that the first of the Domecqs arrived in Jerez to take over the firm to which he was to give his name.

The business was founded in 1730 by an Irishman, Patrick Murphy, who bought vineyards in the Macharnudo and Carrascal districts and made wine in Jerez. He was a bachelor, apparently in frail health, and

34 Butt of sherry at Pedro Domecq dedicated to the King and Queen of Spain

increasingly relied on a friend and neighbour in the Plaza de Plateros, Juan Haurie from the French side of the Pyrenees, to help him. When Murphy died in 1762, he left his entire property, including the vineyards, to Haurie. He too, was a bachelor, but with a drive that Murphy lacked, and set about developing his interests by sending for his five nephews from France. It was unfortunate that when Napoleon invaded Spain in 1808, some fourteen years after the original Haurie had died, the firm was being run by the Francophile Juan Carlos Haurie, who collaborated with Marshal Soult to the extent of provisioning the French troops and levying taxes in the name of the alien French government. When the French were driven out, Haurie found himself responsible for the French government's unpaid debts, and from being the wealthiest and most substantial shipper in Jerez, was left penniless.

It was at this juncture that Pedro Domecq Lembeye came to the rescue. He was the son of the original Haurie's sister, who had married the aristocratic Jean de Domecq. Educated in France and England, he joined Juan Carlos Haurie's English agents as a clerk. They were, however, doing so badly at the time, selling in fact only twenty butts a year, that Haurie asked him to make alternative arrangements, and with a fellow clerk, John James Ruskin and financial backing from a Mr Henry Telford, he set up the firm of Ruskin, Telford and Domecq, which within a few years was selling an annual 3,000 butts. (John James Ruskin was the father of John Ruskin, the writer, who fell in love with one of Pedro Domecq's five daughters by his English wife Diana Lancaster, but was refused by her; all five of the girls later married into the French aristocracy.)

Meanwhile in Jerez things with the Hauries were going from bad to worse. After his arrival in Jerez in 1816, Pedro Domecq by dint of hard work and shrewd management began to turn things around and in 1822 took over most of the vineyards, bodegas and *soleras* of the now bankrupt Haurie and changed the name of the firm to Pedro Domecq. With Juan Sánchez, the most skilled blender in Jerez, as his *capataz* or head cellarman, Pedro Domecq Lembeye built up the company into one of the largest and wealthiest in Jerez. He died a millionaire at fifty-seven in 1839 as the result of an extraordinary accident; when taking treatment for acute rheumatism, he was suspended over a cauldron of steaming water, and the ropes that supported him broke and he was plunged into it.

Pedro Domecq Lembeye was the founder of perhaps the most famous of the sherry dynasties. In Jerez, the family was later to intermarry with those of Diez, La Riva, Bobadilla, González, Williams,

Guerrera, Croft, Rivero, Valdespino, Algar and Vergara; in Puerto de Santa María, with those of Osborne and Caballero; and in Sanlúcar de Barrameda, with Barbadillo, Argueso, Garcia-Monje and Leon Manjón.

The company continued to expand and to prosper under his successors. Juan Pedro Domecq acquired more vineyards in

35 *The* capataz *at Pedro Domecq demonstrating the use of a* venencia

Macharnudo and bought the palace of the Marqués de Montana, now known as the Palacio Domecq as a residence (it is now used only for receptions and banquets). The nephew who succeeded him, Pedro Domecq Loustau, is best known for commercialising Jerez brandy. The present head of the firm, Don José Ignacio Domecq, nicknamed 'The Nose' because of his skill in tasting, is one of the great sherry authorities of his generation, and like most of the family a keen horseman and crack polo player.

Pedro Domecq owns some 1,050 hectares of vineyards in Jerez Superior with very large holdings in the Macharnudo area. It has sixteen bodegas in Jerez and others in Puerto de Santa María housing some 80,000 butts of sherry and 60,000 of brandy. Staff in the bodegas has been reduced from 1,500 to 361 in ten years thanks to modernisation of equipment in the bodegas, and from 100 to 45 in the vineyards. Apart from HIJOS DE AGUSTIN BLAZQUEZ and LA RIVA, S.A. in Jerez, Domecq owns a number of large foreign subsidiaries, of which the largest in Mexico has sales of over 7 million litres of locally produced brandies and imported sherry and table wines. At the time of the sherry depression in 1981, when Domecq lost 782 million pesetas, it was the profits of Domecq Mexico which saved the firm.

Best know of the Domecq sherries is the *fino* 'La Ina', pale with a greenish cast, classic *flor* nose, round and supple with just a trace of sweetness, and entirely consistent. 'Río Viejo' is an outstanding dry *oloroso*, light, dry and fragrant. Other wines include the popular 'Double Century' medium *amontillado*, pale cream and cream, and an older, richer and more mature 'Celebration Cream'. 'Fundador' was the first Jerez brandy to be sold on a large scale, and though sales have declined is still one of the most honest, least caramelised and most to the British taste for a dry brandy. Others include 'Carlos I', 'Carlos III' and the beautiful and mellow old 'Marqués de Domecq'. Domecq, which owns its own distilleries outside Jerez, also produces 'Beefeater' gin under licence in Spain and 'Domecq Domain' and 'Marqués de Arienzo' Rioja from its vineyards in the Rioja Alavesa.

Estévez, S.A., José
P.O. Box 167, Cristal 4, 6 y 8, Jerez.
The successors to the old firm of Félix Ruíz, whose origins date back to 1809, when Don Iñigo Ruíz de Villegas y Sánchez de Tagle began dealing in sherries. The family later constructed bodegas in Jerez and branched into different concerns, trading as A.R. Ruíz Hermanos (the first of the string of firms to be taken over by RUMASA), Félix Ruíz de

Ruíz S.A. and J. Ruíz y Cia. The company maintains stocks of some 10,000 butts and sells both in the domestic market and in Europe and the Americas.

The sherries are sold under the names of 'Don Félix' (*fino, amontillado* and pale cream), 'Ruíz' (*palo cortado*) and also 'El Tutor', 'Tocayo' and 'Don Pancho'. There is also an old 'Tartesio' brandy and an excellent 'Ponche Ruíz' (which is recommended at breakfast – presumably as a hang-over cure!).

Fernández, S.A., Manuel
see Bobadilla y Cia

Findlater, Mackie, Todd & Co. Ltd
Findlater Matta Agencies, Windsor Avenue, Merton Abbey, London SW19 2SN.
This London shipper is famous for its 'Dry Fly'. Alexander Findlater founded a wine business in 1823 and in 1855 went into partnership with Bruce Beverage Todd. The firm began shipping sherry at an early date and now has its own *soleras*, maintained for it in Jerez by a leading producer. The name 'Dry Fly' was first used in the 1930s. Findlater was already using the name 'March brown', a fly used in trout fishing, for a popular brown sherry. A fisherman colleague suggested that the name 'Dry Fly' would admirably describe a light and elegant *fino*, and the firm duly introduced one. When supplies ran out during the last war, the company was also marketing a big-selling 'Findlater's fino', a name that it was impossible to register, and it was decided to rechristen it.

Today's 'Dry Fly' is in fact a crisp and nutty *amontillado* with a hint of sweetness. The *fino*, very dry, delicate and with an aroma of bitter almonds, is now called 'River Fly', while 'May Fly' and 'Lake Fly' describe the firm's *olorosos*, both sweet, the first light and fragrant, and the other, dark, luscious and rich.

Galán, S.A., M. Gil
Ferrocarríl, 14, 11401 Jerez.
Small firm marketing a range of sherries under the names of 'Gil Galán' and 'La Condesa', and also 'Formidable' and 'Solera 1890' brandies.

Garvey, S.A.
P.O. Box 12, Divina Pastora, Jerez.
William Garvey, the founder of the firm, came of an Irish family

descended on his father's side from the Garbhes, Princes of Murrisk in pre-Christian times, and on his mother's, through the Ormonde family, from Edward I of England. In 1776 the young man, then twenty, sailed to Cádiz to buy merino rams for crossing with his father's ewes. It is said that his ship foundered during a violent storm in the bay of Cádiz and that he was rescued by a Captain Rafael Gómez of the Spanish navy, in whose house in Puerto Real near Cádiz he was nursed back to health by the good captain's daughter, Sebastiana, with whom he promptly fell in love. It is not known whether his father ever received the rams, but certain it is that William Garvey later married Sebastiana Gómez, and for this or other reasons, remained in Spain, first settling in Sanlúcar de Barrameda.

His first dealings in wine were in a small way, and the oldest document in the very complete Garvey archives is a receipt dated 1780 made out to one Juan O'Connery for '8,858 and 20 more reales in hard money' (the old-fashioned *real*, still sometimes used notionally in wine transactions to represent a quarter of a peseta, was then, of course, worth far more). At that period he was associated with another Irishman, Richard Shiel and the firm of Devereux, Shiel & Co. in London. In 1793, at the age of thirty-eight, he made the move to Jerez. Though times were difficult, because of recurrent hostilities with England during the Napoleonic period, Garvey laid plans for the erection of the largest bodega in Jerez and also for the elaboration of an entirely new style of wine.

Until 1823, all sherry with few exceptions was a rich, sweetened and golden *oloroso*-type wine. Garvey envisaged the export of a much lighter, drier and straw-coloured sherry – in fact, *fino* as we now know it. Experiments in this direction had been made by Joseph Gordon in 1795, but with little success, and it was to be left to William Garvey's son to export *fino* in quantity.

Patrick Garvey, in common with the great new bodegas, which he completed, and the new wine, 'San Patricio', was named after the patron saint of Ireland. The bodegas were the largest to be completed in Jerez for more than a century and remained so until RUMASA built Bodegas Internacionales in the 1970s. Measuring 166 by 34 metres (588 by 126 ft) with six aisles supported by 150 pillars and comprising 30,000 square metres, its airy arcades accommodated 7,500 butts of sherry. Making full use of the new facilities, during the 1840s and early 1850s Patrick Garvey became the largest shipper of sherries. Thus, in 1843 he shipped 1,851 butts, followed by Pedro Domecq with 1,809; Pemartín, Gordon and Beigbeder were the only others with more than 1,000. Ten years later in 1853, he still led the field with

XVII
'Bodega in Jerez de la
Frontera'; nineteenth-
century engraving

XVIII
*The old bodegas of
Fernando A. de Terry in
Puerto de Santa María*

XIX
*The recently built new
bodegas at the Rancho
Croft*

XX
*The 'Mezquita', the
huge new store built
by Pedro Domecq for
maturing their
brandies*

95,145 arrobas (an arroba is approximately 16 litres), closely pursued by Pedro Domecq with 94,716 and González Dubosc (the predecessors of González Byass) with 91,887. At this same period he brought to fruition his father's plans for the commercialisation of *fino* sherry, amassing stocks of the 'straw' wines by night in the San Patricio bodega to avoid the mockery of his neighbours and first launching them with immediate success through his Dublin agents, James McCullagh.

Affairs continued to prosper under the direction of Patrick Garvey's sons Guillermo and José. They were, however, both bachelors, and on José's death the firm was split up among the numerous members of the family and became a limited company. It thereafter underwent something of eclipse, but came back strongly in the decades following the Spanish Civil War with the acquisition of new vineyards and the construction of the large new Bellavista complex on the outskirts of Jerez for the vinification and stabilisation of the wines, with provision for future storage capacity of 75,000 butts.

The firm was taken over by RUMASA in 1978, who continued with the modernisation of the bodegas, meticulously restored the old family house and stepped up sales of the wine, both in the domestic and foreign markets. After the expropriation of RUMASA, the firm was for a time run by the government and then sold to a German cooperative.

Garvey owns eight vineyards, some 600 hectares in all, radiating like a fan from Jerez in the best Jerez Superior region, of which the largest is the 115-hectare Myriam de Montegil on the main road from Jerez to Seville. The original Guadalete bodegas are among the most impressive in Jerez, with a quarter-of-a-mile long arcade flanking the central patio and housing an oloroso *solera*; the tremendous San Patricio bodega, for long the largest in Jerez; and the Sacristía, bedecked with the flags of all the many countries to which the sherries are exported. Sales of sherry currently amount to some eight million bottles annually, with about the same amount of brandy.

Best-known of the Garvey sherries is the *fino* 'San Patricio', pale, dry, and at its best perhaps a little rounder and softer than 'Tío Pepe' – though I confess to some disappointment with recent samples, which have been somewhat 'earthy'. Other sherries are a crisp and delicate 'La Lidia' *manzanilla*; a nutty old 'Tío Guillermo' *amontillado*; the 'Long Life' medium *oloroso*; a dark, bone-dry and intense old 'Ochavico' *oloroso*; and a mellow 'Flor de Jerez' cream. There is a big-selling 'Espléndido' brandy, a more mature 'Gran Garvey' and the choice old 'Renacimiento'.

XXI

Ceremonial coach and team of Carthusian horses belonging to Bodegas Terry

XXII

Tasting room in the old cellars of Bodegas Terry, Puerto de Santa María

González Byass, S.A.

Manuel Ma. González, 12, Jerez.

Don José Antonio González y Rodrigo was a member of the royal bodyguard, a favourite of the sovereign but with a reputation as a ladykiller, which led to his being appointed Administrator of the Royal Salt Marshes at Sanlúcar de Barrameda – a safe distance from Madrid. There, he settled down and married María del Rosario Angel, who bore him two daughters and five sons. She was left an early widow, but struggled to send four of her sons to university in Seville; the youngest, Manuel María González Angel, was a delicate boy and for reasons of health she placed him in Cádiz with a firm of bankers. At the age of twenty-three he decided that his future lay in the wine trade and in Jerez, where an uncle on his mother's side, José de la Peña, owned a small bodega and helped him to set up in business. It was in gratitude for this that Manuel María later named his best-selling sherry 'Tío Pepe' (this being the Spanish equivalent of 'Uncle Joe'). In his first year he shipped only ten butts and in the next 62, but by 1838 exports amounted to the respectable total of 819, and on the strength of it he married Victorina de Soto y Lavaggi, daughter of a Cádiz merchant of the aristocratic Soto de Briviesca family from Old Castile.

With business expanding rapidly his need was now for finance, and his uncle introduced him to another Sanluqueño, a Sr Gutiérrez de la Aguera, who enabled him to buy a disused vineyard next to the Collegiate Church. It was called La Sacristía, and this was how he named his first large bodega built on the site. The pace of expansion was now so great that Sr Gutiérrez took fright and bowed out. At this juncture Manuel María fell in with Jean Bautista Dubosc, a Catalan of French descent, fluent in languages and a magnificent salesman. The company was renamed González & Dubosc (the name still used by González Byass for its *cava* wine from the Penedès) and while Manuel María devoted his energies to making the sherry, Dubosc toured the world selling it. In 1853 Manuel María was acquiring vineyards and began construction of the great new Constancia bodega, in which he installed the wines in 300-year-old butts with forged iron hoops, which he had acquired from the Dukes of Medinaceli and after which he later named the 'Amontillado del Duque'. By 1855, when the new bodega was completed, exports to England alone were more than 3,000 butts and by 1873 had risen to a peak of 10,409 butts or nearly 7 million bottles, larger than those of any other bodega in Jerez.

But this is looking ahead. Dubosc died in 1859; in 1863 Manuel María took into partnership Robert Blake Byass, his London agent who had been selling the wines with such success in England, and the name

36 Manuel María González Angel, the founder of González Byass

37 *Ancient butts at González Byass, of which the contents are used in minute amount for blending with younger wine*

of the concern was changed to González Byass & Co. The company remained in the hands of the two families until 1988, when the Byasses sold out their interest, and it is now 100 per cent owned by the González family.

The year 1862 was a historic one for González Byass, as it saw the visit of Queen Isabel II to the bodegas and, as a result, the setting up of the famous 'Los Apóstoles'. The Queen had expressed a wish to see the pressing of the grapes, but as it was early October and the harvest was long over, Manuel María's minions set about buying up all the grapes which he could find from peasants who had bought them to keep for eating. They ended up with no less than 23,000 kilograms; the Queen had her demonstration in the splendidly decorated bodegas; and Manuel María, who had spent 30,000 duros on the entertainment, was offered a dukedom for his pains. This he modestly refused, but the wine so strangely made turned out to be of extraordinary quality and was housed in a monster cask of 3,000 gallons specially made in Heidelberg with oak from New Orleans. It held the equivalent of 33 butts, the age of Christ, and was consequently named 'El Cristo' and still survives, flanked by twelve smaller casks or 'Apóstoles' holding examples of the best possible sherries in different styles. A cask representing Judas is kept out of sight in the vinegar store.

Before his death in 1887, Manuel María González had constructed a whole complex of further bodegas, of which the most remarkable was the revolutionary La Concha, built airily of wrought iron by Gustave Eiffel, more than 100 metres in circumference, with a central ring carrying the whole weight of the roof. Manuel María served as a member of the Cortes for Jerez and as Mayor of Sanlúcar, and confounded his doctors by surviving to the age of seventy-five.

He was succeeded as head of the firm by his son Pedro Nolasco González Soto, later to be made Marqués de Torre-Soto de Briviesca by King Alfonso XIII, who went shooting with him and knew him more informally as 'Tío Perico'. Don Pedro, who travelled the Continent selling the wines and was on first name terms with half the crowned heads of Europe, introduced polo and also the first pennyfarthing bicycle to Jerez. My wife has in her possession an amusing letter written by Don Pedro to one of her forebears, Don Pedro Manjón, in Sanlúcar de Barrameda. It reads in translation:

> I am sorry not to have been at the bodega when you called yesterday and also not to have been able to stop when I passed you in the Lanceria, but I am a novice on a bicycle and once I get down I am unable to mount it again, and do not like making an ass of myself.

38 *'The Twelve Apostles' at González Byass, butts containing extremely old and choice wine*

39 *The La Concha bodega of González Byass, an innovative metal structure designed by Gustave Eiffel*

A great collector, in his later days, of bicycles, cars, lottery tickets and pictures, he amassed no less than twenty grand pianos, stored in a disused bodega. He nevertheless found time to preside most successfully over the fortunes of the firm, weathering the disastrous fire of August 1908 and a cataract of 500,000 litres of burning sherry.

It has been said that the Gonzálezes die young – and indeed his son inherited the title of the Marqués de Bonanza because all the more

direct heirs to the title died one after another – but Don Pedro survived into his nineties and was riding a polo pony a year or two before. This son, Manuel María González Gordon, was to become a legend in Jerez, but was a sickly child in the family tradition and his life was despaired of at five months old. What happened after that he tells in the introduction of his classic book *Sherry*:

> My father invited the doctors into an adjoining room and ordered the servants to bring glasses and a bottle of Sherry. As the servant passed in front of us with the decanter on a tray, the sun's rays shining on the golden wine must have caught my eye, because I raised my tiny hand and it occurred to my mother to give me a spoonful of Sherry. This she did, and as I smacked my lips and appeared to relish it she repeated the dose – a 'treatment' she went on giving me for several weeks . . . Only my mother could explain my miraculous recovery . . .

González Byass now owns some 2,000 hectares of vineyards in Jerez Superior. Technically innovative, the firm was the first to pick the grapes into plastic containers, so speeding up delivery to the bodega and avoiding accidental crushing and premature fermentation in the traditional wooden tubs. Its Oenological Investigation Centre and nurseries, where the best and healthiest Palomino is produced by cloning (see page 53), are advanced in their methods. A current share

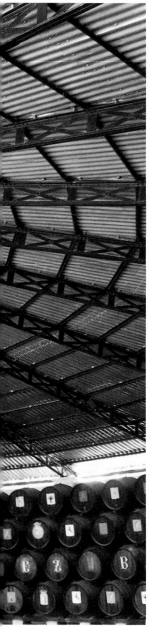

40 *The bodega mice at González Byass, affectionately protected and fed on sherry*

41 *The great modern Las Copas bodega of González Byass, where the wine is vinified*

of some 28 per cent of the world market for sherry has necessitated massive additions to the bodegas and vinification plant in recent decades. The 'Tío Pepe' bodega was planned in 1961 by the Marqués de Torroja and completed six years later by his son. Constructed of reinforced concrete with four domes, each the size of that of St Peter's in Rome, its three floors house 30,000 butts of maturing 'Tío Pepe', the equivalent of 20 million bottles of sherry. Even larger and more modern in design is the great steel and glass 'Las Copas' complex, just outside Jerez on the road to Cádiz, with a capacity for crushing two million kilograms of grapes per day and storage space for 60,000 butts.

Best-known of the González Byass sherries is, of course, 'Tío Pepe', the biggest selling *fino* in the world. Pale in colour, bone-dry, light and

fragrant, it is of consistent high quality. Its freshness, in the United Kingdom at any rate, is achieved by shipping it in nitrogen-capped containers and bottling it in Sheerness, with extreme precautions to avoid oxidation, as the market requires. 'Viña A.B.', named after Sr Andrés Botaina, from whom Manuel María González Angel bought one of his first vineyards, is a splendid example of a *fino amontillado*, aged in *solera* for 10–12 years and for half of its life under *flor*. Other rare and beautiful wines are the old 'Amontillado del Duque', the 'Apóstoles' dry *oloroso* and 'Metusalén' cream. The popular range includes 'Elegante' *fino*, 'La Concha' medium, 'San Domingo' pale cream and 'Nectar' cream. González Byass makes a quartet of brandies, in ascending order of price, 'Soberano', 'Insuperable', 'Conde Duque' and 'Lepanto'. 'Soberano' is one of the best and least caramelised of the inexpensive Jerez brandies, and 'Lepanto', in its cut glass decanter, among the lightest, driest, smoothest and most fragrant.

Gordon, Luís G.
Colon, 2, 11401 Jerez.
This old-established firm was founded in 1754 by Arthur Gordon, one of many members of this Scottish family to establish themselves in Jerez. It therefore preceded by some time and has outlasted the better-known firm founded by C.P. Gordon, who was one of the leading shippers at the beginning of the nineteenth century and whose son became British Vice-Consul in Jerez.

The sherries shipped by Luís G. Gordon include 'La Giralda' *manzanilla*, 'Neluco' *fino*, 'Tambor' *oloroso*, 'Navegante' *palo cortado*, 'Altanero' *amontillado* and 'Royal Crescent' cream.

Guerrero Ortega, José María
Picadueña Alta, 135, Jerez.
Better known as an *almacenista* (see page 115), its sherries are available through EMILIO LUSTAU.

Harvey & Sons (España) Ltd
P.O. Box 494, Arcos, 53, Jerez.
This famous Bristol firm traces its history to 1796, though it was not until 1822 that the first Harvey joined it. Bristol has for centuries been shipping wine and colonial products, and John Harvey's grandfather was a hard-bitten and hard-drinking sea dog, of whom it is related that while sharing a bottle of port one evening, he rang for his servant and motioning to his friend, by now prostrate on the floor, said: 'Kindly remove Mr Prothero and bring me another bottle of port.' He

42 *Harvey's bodegas
in Jerez*

43 *Mississippi
alligators in the
grounds of Harveys*

subsequently perished in an Atlantic hurricane, together with his wife and entire ship's company. Unlike his father, also a captain, John Harvey refused to go to sea and instead joined his uncle's wine business in Denmark Street, eventually taking it over and renaming it John Harvey.

Like the other Bristol firms, Harveys bought wines in Jerez and shipped them to Bristol for blending in its extensive cellars. This, for almost a century, was how the famous 'Bristol Cream' was produced, the sherries coming from a variety of suppliers, notably Cuvillo of Puerto de Santa María and, later on, from José María Ruíz Mateos, who built up RUMASA on the profits of an exclusive contract. This was rescinded, and at about the time that Harveys was merged with Allied Brewers, the company looked about for its own source of supply and bought the old-established Jerez house of Mackenzie in 1970. It thus acquired a bodega, 4,000 butts of sherry and 40 hectares of vineyards, soon to be supplemented by another 400 at Gibalbín north of Jerez owned jointly with ANTONIO BARBADILLO of Sanlúcar. The two companies also constructed a brand-new vinification plant embodying the latest in continuous presses and temperature-controlled fermentation vats. Harveys next went shares with GARVEY in developing another 400 hectares of vineyards, which it has subsequently taken over, and in 1979 bought from RUMASA the bodegas of the Marqués de Misa, adjoining those of Mackenzie. The property is now one of the most impressive in Jerez with the noble arcaded bodegas set amongst wide green lawns and trees, with a legacy from Mackenzie in the shape of a pool containing a couple of Mississippi alligators.

After the failure of its erstwhile trading partner, RUMASA, Harveys in 1985 bought from the Spanish government the two important firms of PALOMINO & VERGARA and TERRY. Apart from the acquisition of further extensive vineyards, bodegas and wineries, and a string of new labels, this has gained the company a distribution network in Spain and access through Terry to the all-important Spanish brandy market. It is claimed that, as a result of these latest acquisitions, Harveys is now the world's largest sherry company.

All this seems a far cry from the turn of the century, when the Prince of Wales, shortly to become Edward VII, remarked of 'Bristol Cream' that 'All I can say is, you must have dam' fine cows.' Smooth, luscious and sweet, it is now the best-selling sherry not only in the important UK, US and German markets, but in the world as a whole. Other big-selling Harvey sherries are 'Luncheon Dry' *fino*, 'Club Amontillado' (in fact a medium sherry), 'Finesse' pale cream, and

'Tico', a light sherry specially blended for drinking on the rocks with tonic, lemonade or soda. At the top end of the range Harveys have recently introduced four excellent wines: '1796 Manzanilla' (made for Harveys by Antonio Barbadillo), '1796 Superior Fino', '1796 Fine Old Amontillado' and '1796 Palo Cortado'; the 'Palo Cortado' especially is a really first-rate old wine, fragrant, full-bodied, intense in flavour and very long on finish. See also PALOMINO & VERGARA, S.A. and TERRY, S.A.

Hidalgo, S.A., Emilio M.
P.O. Box 221, Calle Clavel, 29, Jerez.
An independent family company which still operates from bodegas in the Calle Clavel, first established in 1874 and later extended and modernised. It owns 140 hectares of vines in Añina and Carrascal and began vinifying its wines in 1926. Stocks amount to some 8,000 butts. Its sherries include 'Hidalgo' *manzanilla* and *fino*, 'Tresillo' *amontillado*, 'Magistrál' cream; and there is also an old 'Privilegio' brandy.

Internacionales S.A., Bodegas
P.O. Box 300, Crtra Madrid–Cádiz, km 641·7, Jerez.
Bodegas Internacionales was one of the most ambitious ventures of José María Ruíz Mateos and RUMASA. The huge complex, the largest single winery in Jerez, embodies a bodega of 50,000 square metres under one roof housing more than 60,000 butts, a state of the art vinification plant and laboratories, a spacious office block and large gardens. It was built not only to make sherries under its own label, but to service and make the wines for six old-established firms taken over by RUMASA and separately described. These were M. MISA, S.A.; J. PEMARTIN Y CIA, S.A.; BERTOLA, S.A.; VARELA, S.L.; DIESTRO, S.A. and CARLOS DE OTAOLAURRUCHI, S.A.

Under the Presidency of Don Beltrán Domecq the company developed the excellent range of 'Duke of Wellington' sherries, comprising a dry and elegant *fino*, and an *amontillado*, pale cream and cream.

After the expropriation of RUMASA in 1983, the company was first run by the Spanish government and sold in 1985 to Don Marcos Eguizábal, who also operates large bodegas in the Rioja. Under his regime further huge extensions are being made, with further batteries of giant stainless steel tanks being installed for the vinification and storage of the must.

The firm of DIEZ-MERITO also belongs to the group, but it possesses its own bodegas and *soleras* in Jerez and a large modern vinification and bottling plant outside the town, and operates as a separate unit.

La Riva, S.A..
Alvar Núñez, 44, Jerez.
Founded in 1776, this small but prestigious bodega is one of the oldest-established in Jerez. It was bought by Pedro Domecq in the 1970s, but is still managed by the de la Riva family, one of whose forbears in the nineteenth century is credited with introducing the *deserpia*, or boxing of individual vines with a shallow pit so as to catch the winter rain. The bodega owns 53 hectares of vineyard in the best Macharnudo area and some of the choicest old *soleras* in Jerez. 'Tres Palmas', one of the most famous of *finos*, is pale, medium-bodied, intense in nose and flavour, bone-dry with clean acidity at the end. Hugh Johnson has remarked that some of the old *solera* wines, such as the 'Oloroso 1830', are so concentrated as to be almost painful to drink. The nutty 'Guadalupe' is an authentic dry *amontillado*, and there is a first-rate *palo cortado*.

Lagos, S.A., B.M.
P.O. Box 440, Crtra de Sanlúcar, s/n, Jerez.
Founded in 1910, the company is now part-owned by JOSE MEDINA & CIA and part by the Cologne-based West German group of Gedelfi. This was the first investment of German capital in Jerez, and the company is one of the largest exporters of sherry to West Germany in what is becoming an increasingly important market. The main brand is the 'Tío Nico' range of sherries, and the firm also makes an 'Emperador' brandy.

Luque, S.A., M. Gil
Crtra Arcos, km 2, 11406 Jerez.
Small firm marketing a range of 'Deportivo' sherries.

Lustau, S.A., Emilio
P.O. Box 193, Plaza del Cubo, 4, Jerez.
Emilio Lustau, founded in 1896, is one of the largest independent family-owned firms and among the top seven sherry exporters. It owns vineyards in the Balbaina and Raboatun areas, and its main bodegas are in the heart of Jerez on either side of the Moorish city wall, which forms an integral part of some of them. One bodega, in fact, which lacks the normal pillars and has a high, vaulted roof, is thought to have been the headquarters of the city guard in Moorish times. To

accommodate expanding production, the firm has constructed very large new bodega buildings in its oldest vineyard, Nuestra Señora de la Esperanza, in the hills of the Raboatun Alto to the north of the town.

Lustau have for long prospered by shipping good quality sherries for selling under their customers' labels. They also market a complete range of quality sherries from *manzanilla* to cream labelled as 'Lustau'. But this is only the half of it. There is a range of 14 Emilio Lustau Reserva sherries, including a top-flight 'Peninsula' *palo cortado*; the very rare 'Emperatriz Eugenia' *oloroso*, bone-dry, intense to a degree with endless finish; a luscious 100 per cent Pedro Ximénez; and a dense, raisiny 'Solera Reserva Emelin' moscatel, as much like a Málaga as a sherry. Then there is an old 'East India' cream, matured in the way of the old madeiras by being shipped to and from the tropics in the hold of a ship (see also pages 85–87); but what has particularly caught the imagination of sherry drinkers is the *almacenista* range. These are small parcels of wines, often from individual vineyards, held and matured by stockholders who normally sell them only to the commercial bodegas for improving their blends. They were rarely seen abroad until Lustau began selecting, bottling and shipping them for retail sale. A complete list of their suppliers, whose names appear on the labels, is given under ALMACENISTAS.

Marqués del Real Tesoro, Herederos del
P.O. 27, Pajarete, 3, Jerez.
In 1760 H.E. Don Joaquín Manuel de Villena, Gualfajara, Rodríguez de Manzano y Nieto, Lieutenant-General in the Royal Spanish Navy, was in command of a fleet carrying bullion from South America to Spain, when it was attacked by pirates. In the ensuing encounter the General's ship ran out of ammunition. In addition to gold destined for the Royal Treasury, she was also carrying silver bought on Don Joaquín's own account. This he now had melted down and made into cannonballs, and the pirates were repulsed. In gratitude, King Charles III created him Marqués del Real Tesoro, or Marquis of the Royal Treasure.

Generations later, in 1904, the Marquis's grandson, Don Juan Jácome y Pareja, Vice-Admiral and Minister of Marine, founded the bodega on the basis of large stocks of sherry bought from the Conde de Villacreces and laid down two centuries before. It therefore started with *soleras* containing some of the finest wine in Jerez. The bodega in Jerez houses 5,000 butts and another in Sanlúcar de Barrameda, 2,000. The firm has maintained a high reputation and is particularly well known for its *manzanillas* and 'Viejo' *amontillado*, an authentic wine, dry and nutty, and not a 'medium' sherry. The nautical origins of its founders are picturesquely portrayed in the picture of a galleon on the label of the 'Almirante' brandy, and Real Tesoro also makes a good *ponche*.

Misa, S.A., M.

P.O. Box 300, Crtra Madrid–Cádiz, km 641·7, Jerez.

In 1844 at the age of twenty-nine, Manuel Misa, who came of a seafaring family from Bayona in Galicia, established an export firm in Jerez and travelled Europe and America selling his wines, which included 'Gran Solera 1815', 'Abolengo', 'Reañejo' and 'Waterloo'. They were of good quality and he was soon selling them in large amount. Public benefactor and member of the Cortes for Jerez, he was created Conde de Bayona in 1882 and Marqués de Misa and a grandee of Spain in 1889. He was well known in London, where he became President of the Spanish Chamber of Commerce and presented to the Spanish Government the magnificent Embassy building in Belgrave Square, fully furnished and equipped.

The firm grew into one of the most prosperous and substantial in Jerez, and in 1899 stocks amounted to 13·1 million litres and 76 different types of wine. It was one of those absorbed by RUMASA, who transferred the *soleras* to BODEGAS INTERNACIONALES and continued making wines under the Misa label; the bodega itself, one of the most impressive in Jerez with its lofty and graceful arches, was sold to Harvey's. Following the downfall of RUMASA, BODEGAS INTERNACIONALES under its new management still markets Misa brands, of which the best-known are 'Chiquilla' *fino*, 'Abolengo' *amontillado*, 'La Novia' *oloroso* and the 'Royal' brandy, very popular in Madrid and the central area of Spain.

Núñez, Antonio

P.O. Box 349, Ronda del Caracol, s/n, Jerez.

A small family firm, founded in 1927 by Don Antonio Núñez. It makes a range of sherries and brandies, the main labels being 'Santacuna' and 'Arrumbador', and also controls the historic firm of J.M. Rivero.

Palomino & Vergara, S.A.

P.O. Box 1, Colon, 1, Jerez.

The Palomino family claim descent from Fernán Yanez Palomino, a knight of Alfonso X, who wrested Jerez from the Moors in 1264, and is said to have given his name to the Palomino grape. The family was certainly engaged in the wine trade from the thirteenth century onwards as owners of vineyards and makers of wine. The Vergara family, too, have a long history of wine-making and established a business for maturing and shipping sherry in Puerto de Sta María in 1765. The name of the firm was changed successively to Vergara & Dickinson and Juan Vicente Vergara, before joining forces with that of Palomino under the banner of Palomino & Vergara. In 1963 it was taken over by RUMASA, the beautiful family house of the Vergara family in its decorative gardens, La Atalaya, becoming the executive headquarters of RUMASA's sherry group (it is now the municipal museum). After the expropriation of RUMASA, Palomino & Vergara was bought from the government by Harveys of Bristol.

44 'The Bank of England' at Palomino & Vergara, where customers come to settle bills and suppliers to be paid

144

45 *La Atalaya, once the Vergara family mansion, then headquarters of RUMASA's wine division, and now the principal museum of Jerez*

The company owns some 300 hectares of vineyards, and the bodegas in the heart of Jerez occupy 35,000 square metres and house 32,000 butts of sherry. The offices are among the most elegant in the place, the balconied ground floor with its great glass dome, marble floor, mahogany counters and gilt cashiers' windows being known as 'The Bank of England'. Above are executive offices and a reception room in art nouveau style with cane furniture and colourful cartoons of flamenco dancers on the walls.

Palomino & Vergara has export markets in Germany and elsewhere, but has not in recent years exported to the United Kingdom, and its attraction to its new owners, Harvey's, evidently lay in its strong position in the domestic market. Its best known sherry (now available in the UK) is the classic 'Tío Mateo' *fino*, dry with good *flor* nose and resembling a *manzanilla* in its lightness. There is an 'Infante' *oloroso*, light, dry and with a good after-taste; the firm is also well-known for its 'Fabuloso' and 'Eminencia' brandies.

Paz, S.A., Luís
Jardinillo, 2, Jerez.
This old family business was jointly bought in 1979 by the Medina family (see MEDINA Y CIA, S.A., JOSE) and the Dutch Ahold B.V., whose chain of Albert Heijn stores are among the largest retailers of sherry in Holland. As a result, Luís Paz is the largest exporter of sherry to Holland and is fast expanding. Best-known of its sherries is the 'Conqueror' range.

Pemartín y Cia, S.A.
P.O. Box 300, Crtra Madrid–Cádiz, km 641·7, Jerez.
Pemartín, a famous name in Jerez, still exists as one of the labels of BODEGAS INTERNACIONALES.

Julián Pemartín was born in Oloron in 1771 and made a large fortune from mining in Mexico. In 1815 he settled in Spain, took out Spanish nationality and in 1819 founded the sherry company of Pemartín y Cia and planted the Cerro Nuevo vineyard. The firm prospered and soon established a virtual monopoly in the United States, where its white-painted butts with scarlet hoops became a familiar sight and the custom was to ask for a 'Pemartín' rather than sherry. Unfortunately, his eldest son, Julián, who inherited the business, was wildly extravagant with a taste for high life and commissioned from the most fashionable architect in France, Garnier, a palace in the style of the Paris opera house, Las Cadenas, as it was called, and the balls and the receptions which he gave there ruined him. He was declared bankrupt in 1879 and his assets were acquired by his London agents Sandeman & Co. in association with Walter J. Buck, sportsman and nature-lover, who took up residence in Las Cadenas. The firm was reorganised as Sandeman, Buck & Co. On the death of Buck's son in the First World War, his daughters, Violet and Dolly, sold their shares to Sandeman's, who then renamed the company Sandeman Hermanos y Cia.

The other two sons of the original Julián Permartín, less profligate than their brother, escaped bankruptcy and carried on business in the name of Pemartín, the firm eventually being merged with RUMASA and hence coming within the orbit of its present owners, BODEGAS INTERNACIONALES.

Its best-known labels are 'Vina Pemartín' *fino* and *amontillado*, '810' and 'Numancia' brandies, and 'Anís del Racimo'.

Rayón, S.A., Bodegas
P.O. Box 178, Rayón 1–3, Jerez.
The firm was founded in 1926 by Don Luís de la Calle Ruíz and remained until very recently in the hands of his widow and children, but has been taken over by ANTONIO NUÑEZ. It makes a range of sherries and a brandy by scrupulous artisan methods.

Rivero, J.M.
Sancho Vizcaíno, 16, Jerez.
The oldest sherry house of which written records exist is that of J.M. Rivero, now controlled by ANTONIO NÚÑEZ.

The earliest of the documents in its possession is one initialled 'C.Z.' by Don Pedro Alonso Cabeza de Aranda y Zarco. CZ became the first brand name in Jerez and survives today. One of his descendants, Don Antonio Cabeza de Aranda y Guzman, Marqués de Montana, took into partnership Don Francisco Antonio Tixera. The firm was then renamed Cabeza y Tixera and passed from him to his son-in-law, Don Pedro Agustín Rivero, of a family originally from Portugal, which settled in Jerez during the sixteenth century and had for long been exporting its wines.

The Rivero family have maintained the historic CZ brand ever since, and their sherries were prized above all others during the eighteenth century. Thus, a plaintive letter of January 1757 from a Nicolás Anso of Cádiz entreats that *'por Dios y mi dinero'* ('in the name of God and my money') he may be done the honour of being sent a barrel of wine, and the firm's archives contain a great deal of fascinating historical incident. At the time of the Battle of Trafalgar a cargo of their sherry was captured and auctioned in Tarifa, only to be recovered by the Riveros and used as a basis for their 'Trafalgar 1805' *soleras*. In 1906, at the instigation of King Alfonso XIII, Don Joaquín Ma. Rivero visited the Court of Edward VII to promote the sales of sherry; the firm still preserves an uncashed cheque from Buckingham Palace and also a later letter of thanks from George V's butler.

In the El Salvador bodega of Rivero there are still treasured 100 arrobas of the famous 'Caveza 1770' and the 'Marqués de Montana 1750'. The firm markets a first-rate range of sherries, if not quite as antique as these, including CZ 'Pale Dry', 'Medium' and 'Oloroso'; the appropriately named 'Trafalgar' cream, dark, sweet, velvety and full-bodied; and also a 'Trafalgar' brandy.

Sánchez Romate Hnos, S.A.
P.O. Box 5, Lealas 26–30, Jerez.

This old-established firm was founded in 1781 by Don Juan Sánchez de la Torre, well-known as a businessman and philanthropist; the Romate family later came into the business through marriage. Now owned by a small consortium, the company remains independent. It owns four vineyards of some 80 hectares in all, two in Macharnudo and one in Balbaina on *albariza* soil, and another in the Cuartillo area on *barro*. Its picturesque old bodegas in the centre of Jerez house some 8,000 butts.

The sherries have long been noted for their quality, and Sánchez Romate were awarded a Royal Warrant by King Alfonso XIII and are still suppliers to the Spanish royal family; they have also been purveyors to the House of Lords and the Vatican. There is a wide range, including *manzanilla*, *fino* and *oloroso*, each in three different qualities. the 'N.P.U.' (Non Plus Ultra) *amontillado* is a dry and unblended *solera* wine of great character, and the 'Iberia' a fine old cream blended from *oloroso* and Pedro Ximénez.

Sánchez Romate is, however, most famous for its 'Cardenal Mendoza' brandy (labelled 'Cardinal' in the United States), a *gran reserva* named after Pedro González de Mendoza, humanist and statesman at the time of the Catholic Monarchs, who became Archbishop of Toledo and primate of Spain in 1482. The brandy was first produced in 1887 and is double-distilled, then aged for some years in oak casks previously used for *oloroso* before going to the *solera*. Smooth and fragrant with a touch of sweetness and suggestion of *oloroso*, it is available in very limited amount (less than 50,000 casks are produced annually), most of it being exported.

Sandeman-Coprimar, S.A.
P.O. Box 53, Pizarro, 10, Jerez.

George Sandeman, founder of the famous House of Sandeman, was born in Perth in 1765. With the loan of £300 from his father he set up in the wine business in London in 1790, writing to his sister that he would return to Perth if he had not made a modest fortune within nine years. Already by 1792 he was dealing in port and had begun to

46 *Butts of* raya *maturing in the sun at Sandeman's bodegas*

represent the important Cádiz sherry house of James Duff in London. Thereafter, and despite the Napoleonic Wars, he was always on the move in Spain and Portugal developing the firm's interests; and in 1809 one of his partners, James Gordon, took up residence in Cádiz and began shipment of sherries under the Sandeman label.

In 1823 Sandeman began obtaining their sherries from the firm of Pemartín and continued doing so until 1879, when, as a result of his extravagances, the son of the original Julián Pemartín (see PEMARTIN Y CIA, S.A.) was bankrupted. In partnership with Walter

J. Buck and trading as Sandeman, Buck & Co., Sandeman took over all Pemartín's assets, including the vineyards, bodegas and *soleras*. For the first time, they were therefore making their own wine in Jerez, and during the First World War bought out Buck's heirs, thus becoming sole owners. Another important purchase was that in 1894 of 800 butts of fine *oloroso* from Antonio Bernardo de Quirós, which were used to found the *soleras* for the now classic 'Royal Corregidor' and 'Imperial Corregidor'.

The House of Sandeman remained under family control until 1980, when it was bought by Seagram. David Sandeman of the sixth generation continues as chairman.

Sandeman now own fifteen vineyards, all in the *albariza* area, amounting to some 650 hectares. The vinification plant is situated a short distance outside Jerez in the Cerro Viejo vineyard inherited from Pemartín. Until as recently as 1981, 70 per cent of the wine was fermented in butts (subsequently passed on to the Distillers' Company for maturing whisky) and the balance in cement *tinajas*. The butts have now been replaced by a battery of 20,000-litre fibreglass-polyester tanks, and the plant is undergoing modernisation with the installation of new presses. The handsome main bodega is in the centre of Jerez, and between this and others the company maintains stocks amounting to 54,000 butts. It is among the top five sherry exporters, shipping to more than 120 countries, the most important markets being Holland, West Germany and the United Kingdom.

Over recent years there have been changes in the style and labelling of the *finos*, the very pleasant 'Apitiv' and, after it, 'Dry Don' having been replaced by 'Don Fino' and 'Dry Fino'. 'Royal Ambrosante' is a rare and delicious old *palo cortado*; 'Character Amoroso' is a new introduction proceeding from a *solera* laid down in 1895, a light, pale golden *oloroso* with a lovely nutty nose, some sweetness in the middle, but dry at the finish; and 'Armada' remains one of the best and roundest of cream sherries. The 'Royal Corregidor' and 'Imperial Corregidor', which take their name from the El Corregidor vineyard and are made in *soleras* with 14 scales, are magnificent wines, among the best of old *olorosos*, and there is a gorgeous and even older 'Solera 1860', of which only about fifty cases remain.

Soto, S.A., José de
P.O. Box 29, Ma. Antonia Jesús Tirado, 5, Jerez.
One of the surviving family firms, this was founded in 1834 by José de Soto y Entresoto and is best known for being the first to make *ponche*, a digestif usually presented in an eye-catching silvered bottle and made

from a blend of old sherry and brandy, sweetened and flavoured with orange and herbs. It remains one of the best.

Apart from inventing *ponche*, the second of the de Sotos, José de Soto Ruíz, took the lead in combating the phylloxera epidemic, which engulfed Jerez in 1894, by being the first to eschew palliatives, such as injections with carbon disulphide, and rooting up and replanting his Santa Isabel vineyard with American root stocks, subsequently grafted with the native Palomino. De Soto currently has six *albariza* vineyards of some 150 hectares in all: Santa Isabel and La Carrena in Macharnudo; and Calderín de Obispo, La Esperanza, La Rabia and La Carpintera in the Balbaina area. Stocks of maturing sherry amount to 10,000 butts.

It is a pity that the delicious *ponche*, though available in the United Kingdom, is not better known; de Soto sherries, at least, are drunk and appreciated. They include 'Campero' and 'Fino Soto' *finos*; 'La Espuela' *oloroso*; a traditional, dry 'Uvita' *amontillado* and a 'Don Jaime' medium, slightly sweetened for British tastes; and a sweet Soto Cream made with Moscatel and Pedro Ximénez.

Valdespino, S.A., A.R.
P.O. Box 22, Pozo Olivar, 11, Jerez.

Don Alonso Valdespino, from Santander in the north of Spain, was one of the knights who fought by the side of Alfonso X ('The Wise') during the reconquest of Jerez from the Moors in 1264 and participated in the grant of the reoccupied lands. The family had been growers and *almacenistas* since the fourteenth century, when, at the age of twenty in 1837, Antonio Fernández de Valdespino entered the export market. In 1899 the firm expanded by buying that of Heyward, Wilson & Co., whose bodega in Jerez they had stocked with Valdespino wines (Valdespino was long represented in England by Wilson & Valdespino Ltd until the English end of the business was bought out).

Valdespino owns the famous Inocente Valdespino vineyard in the Macharnudo district, together with 'El Corregidor Viejo' and San Isidro in Carrascal. The headquarters of the firm in the centre of Jerez comprises six small bodegas, occupying in all 40,000 square metres and interspersed with charming vine-trellised patios. The oldest was once the part of a convent used for storing grain and olive oil, and the seventeenth-century Bodega del Inocente contains a lofty copper still at least a century old (the Valdespinos have been distilling wine for drinking as brandy since the fifteenth century). A quaint feature is the massive keys to the bodegas, of which the part inserted into the lock is cut in the shape of the number corresponding to the bodega. There are no duplicates, and on a recent visit to the bodegas it was a question of waiting until the truck-driver returned with them!

The methods of the bodega are strictly traditional. The wines are still fermented in cask (Miguel Valdespino commented that 'usually we get very good wines – and occasionally a cask of very good vinegar') and the transfer of wine from one butt to another is still done entirely by hand with a *canoa* and *rocíador* without the use of pumps.

All of the wines are very high quality. 'Montana' and 'Deliciosa' are crisp young *manzanillas* from the firm's bodega in Sanlúcar de Barrameda; the single-vineyard 'Inocente' from a *solera* with no less than ten scales is one of the classic *finos* with pronounced *flor* nose; 'Tio Diego' is a dry, dark and macho *amontillado*, while of the rare 'Don Tomás' *amontillado* I have the following note: 'Light orange-brown. Extremely aromatic nose – hazelnuts, bitter almonds, orange peel. Shut your eyes and you could be back in a bodega in Jerez. Absolutely bone-dry. Long, lingering finish – with a touch of phenol like Laphroaig whisky. Magnificent.' The 'Pedro Ximénez Solera Superior' is intensely sweet and raisiny and perfect for that Jerezano speciality *helado de pasas al Pedro Ximénez* (raisin ice cream).

Varela, S.L.
P.O. 300, Crtra Madrid–Cádiz, km, 641·7, Jerez.
Founded in Puerto de Santa María in 1850 by Don Ramón Jiménez Varela, the firm was bought by RUMASA in 1960 and later incorporated into BODEGAS INTERNACIONALES, which still, under new management, makes and markets its wines, of which the Dry, Medium and especially the Cream are popular in the United Kingdom.

Vergara, S.A., Juan Vicente
P.O. Box 9, Crtra Cartuja s/n, Jerez.
The three Vergara y Vegas brothers, Juan, Bartolomé and Mateo, began business in Puerto de Santa María in 1765. At the beginning of the nineteenth century the business moved to Jerez and split up into the firms of José Joaquín Vergara (later to become Javier Vergara Gordon) and Juan Vicente Vergara. The Vergara family also joined forces with the Palominos to form PALOMINO & VERGARA.

The bodega is now located on a site of 40,000 square metres just outside Jerez and makes a complete range of sherries under the labels of 'JV', 'Fiverlac', 'Fernando de Liñán', 'Ronda', 'El Patio' and, in honour of the British, a pale cream called 'Royal Wedding'.

47 *The famous Inocente Valdespino vineyard in the Macharnudo district*

48 *The massive keys to the different bodegas at Valdespino. The number of each bodega forms part of the key*

Viñas, S.L.
Lealas 28, 11404, Jerez.
The firm are shippers of a complete range of 'Conquistador' sherries.

Williams & Humbert Ltd
P.O. Box 23, Nuño de Cañas, 1, Jerez.
Alexander Williams was a hard-working and ambitious clerk with the

sherry firm of WISDOM & WARTER when he fell in love with Amy Humbert. She was on a visit to Jerez from England and had a brother, Arthur Humbert, learning the business with the firm, whose principal, Joseph Warter, was a close friend of their father. The couple married, and in due course Alexander Williams put it to Warter that he should become a partner. He was summarily, not to say rudely turned down, and at this point his father-in-law came to the rescue by advancing him £1,000 to set up his own business on condition that his son, Arthur Humbert, should become a partner when sufficiently experienced.

49 *The main bodega of Williams & Humbert*

The venture was a success from the start, with Williams first renting part of a bodega and a friend, Edward Engelbach, selling the wines in London. The first was 'Pando', a fresh *fino-amontillado* of the type pioneered by William Garvey, originally shipped in 1878 and popular ever since. Alexander Williams' greatest success was, however, in launching 'Dry Sack' in 1906, a careful blend of *amontillado* and a light *oloroso* with a little Pedro Ximénez to give it a touch of sweetness, which has become one of the world's leading brands and the all-out leader in the 'medium' category.

Development of the firm continued under the redoubtable Charles Williams, a contemporary and friend of Winston Churchill at Harrow and a leading figure in Jerez, founder of the tennis club and *The Monthly Jerez Rag*. In 1972, RUMASA, in search of an international brand, bought the company for a sum reputed to be a thousand million pesetas (or some $16 million). 'Dry Sack' continues to be a name to conjure with, and since the expropriation in 1983, José María Ruíz-Mateos has through thick and thin maintained that the title to the name is his personally, long preventing the government from selling the company. With a court case in England going against him, it has now been sold to ANTONIO BARBADILLO of Sanlúcar de Barrameda.

It is certainly an attractive proposition. Its *albariza* vineyards in Carrascal, Balbaina and Los Tercios, together with the new Santa Lucía vineyard, reputedly the largest single property in the Jerez Superior, amount to 588 hectares, producing an annual 10,000 to 12,000 butts, or some 5 to 6 million litres of must, representing 55 per cent of production. The main bodega is set in wide green lawns, at one corner of which are the extensive stables for the horses used to draw the gleaming carriages on parade during the Vendimia festival and Jerez horse show. Another show-piece is the Bodega de Añadas with butts of vintage wine dating from 1920 to 1986, harvested from the company's different vineyards.

Production facilities have recently been modernised with the installation of modern continuous presses, and all the wine is now fermented in temperature-controlled stainless steel tanks. Between the main bodega in the Calle Nuño de Cañas and three others the company produces 2,500,000 cases of sherry a year, which go to markets in the United States (where 'Dry Sack' is the Number 2 brand), Canada, Europe and the Far East.

'Pando' is now-a-days a dry *fino*, pale with a greenish cast and fresh *flor* nose, mouthfilling and with a hint of bitter almonds at the finish. The 'Dos Cortados' *palo cortado*, from a *solera* of 396 butts, has a deep, dry, nutty nose. Supple, full and fresh in taste, it is more of a light *oloroso* than an *amontillado*. 'Dry Sack' has more of an amontillado nose and is a little sweet and bland in the middle, but of very good quality for such a large-selling wine. 'Walnut Brown', a rich old cream, *does* have an aroma of walnuts and is raisiny and a touch sweet at the end. It is particularly appreciated in Scotland and Canada. The premium quality 'Canasta Cream' is amber-coloured with a taste of clean Pedro Ximénez (in fact from Montilla) and less thick in body than many old creams of its age.

Wisdom & Warter Ltd
Box 20, Pizarro, 7, Jerez.

In September 1854, Joseph Warter left the firm of Haurie, where he had been working, to set up his own business, with a Mr Henry Wisdom selling the wines, acquired in the first place from the old Ysasi bodegas, in London. The firm prospered and was commended by Henry Vizetelly in his 1876 *Facts about Sherry* for the admirable quality of its *finos* and *amontillados*. The odd-sounding name became well-known in England, and *Punch*'s quip that 'Warter makes the wine and Wisdom sells it' has passed into history. Only six years after the firm was founded it ranked tenth on the list of shippers with exports of 949 butts to England, and Joseph Warter also pioneered sales in Holland, now sherry's second largest market. His house in the Avenida Capuchinos was one of the most hospitable in Jerez, renowned for its tennis parties and musical evenings; he was also a great sportsman, and his stables of hunters and race horses still survive at the bodegas.

After a long and honourable history, the firm was bought by González Byass around 1929 and is 100 per cent owned by them, its present Chairman being Don Jaime González-Gordon Diez, younger brother of Don Mauricio of the parent firm.

The company owns some 70 hectares of vineyards in Jerez Superior, including La Bodogonera in Los Tercios, the best *fino* district near the sea, which supplies some one and a half thousand butts annually of highest quality *fino*. The firm's picturesque old bodegas are in the heart of Jerez near those of Valdespino. Many of the workers, as in the vineyards, are in the fourth consecutive generation with Wisdom.

Fermentation takes place in fibreglass-epoxy tanks, the temperature being controlled by the addition of fresh must. The largest market is the United Kingdom, where Wisdom & Warter supply *fino* to Sainsburys, *manzanilla* to Tesco and a full range of 'Don Ramos' own-brand sherries to Unwin's. Holland is another important market, as is Norway, where the firm's agent is the great-grandson of Mr Jans

Rolfsen, who over a century ago first sold Wisdom wines in the country.

There is a full range of sherries and brandy. My notes on some of them are:

'Fino Olivar'. Pale yellow. Fresh and fragrant nose. Very dry with long bitter almond finish.

'Royal Palace' *amontillado*. Intense, nutty *amontillado* nose. Very dry with deep and beautiful finish.

'Merecedor' *oloroso*. Bright amber colour. Clean, light and intense in flavour. Long finish.

'Wisdom's Choice' cream. Light mahogany colour, bright. Fragrant nose. Light and uncloying for a cream and not too sweet. Delicious hint of Moscatel at end.

'Tizón' *oloroso*. A fine *oloroso*, orange-brown, intense nose, light, dry, long finish. A lovely old wine.

50 *Nineteenth-century ledger at Wisdom & Warter with entries for the composition of sherries supplied to Cockburn & Campbell and other Scottish customers*

157

Puerto de Santa María

Bodegas 501
Valdés, 5, 11500 Puerto de Santa María.
Known until recently as Carlos y Javier de Terry, the firm was started in the late nineteenth century by the Terry family, originally of Irish descent, another branch of which founded the larger FERNANDO A. DE TERRY. The original *soleras* dated from 1782 and were acquired from Manuel Moreno de Mora. The company markets a range of sherries under the labels of '501 Marinero' and '501 Tercios', and is well-known for its brandy, also made by a subsidiary in Colombia.

John William Burdon
P.O. Box 6, San Francisco, 32, Puerto de Santa María.
John William Burdon was one of the most successful British sherry shippers and in 1854 shipped more wine than any other bodega. He began as a clerk for Duff Gordon and left to set up his own business, taking over the Harmony bodegas in Puerto de Santa María. His impressive establishment in the middle of Puerto de Santa María now serves as stables for the Carthusian horses of Bodegas Terry. He married into a local family, but there were no children, and on his death the business was sold to Luís de la Cuesta, in turn bought in

51 Fino *solera at Luís Caballero in Puerto de Santa María*

159

1932 by LUIS CABALLERO, which continues to market a variety of sherries under the Burdon label. These include a crisp and fresh 'Dry Fino'; a 'Medium Amontillo'; a 'Pale Cream'; and a full-bodied and raisiny 'Rich Cream'.

Caballero, S.A., Luís

P.O. Box 6, San Francisco, 32, Puerto de Santa María.

The Caballeros, originally from Vigo, entered the wine trade in Chipiona in 1795 and became shippers in 1830 after the purchase of the bodegas of the Dukes of Medinaceli and their invaluable *soleras* of *amontillado* and *oloroso* dating from the seventeenth century. The San Bartolomé bodega, with a roof supported by timbers from old sailing ships, was once a tithe barn and part of it was used for the stables of the Dukes of Medinaceli. Their former palace, the Moorish Castle of San Marcos, also belongs to Caballero; recently restored, it is now used for banquets and receptions.

Under the chairmanship of Don Luís Caballero, one of the most forceful protagonists of sherry, the company is 100 per cent controlled by him; his two brothers, responsible respectively for vineyards and real estate; and his three sisters. In 1932 it bought the firms of JOHN WILLIAM BURDON and LA CUESTA and still markets a wide range of sherries under their brand names.

There are 300 hectares of vineyards, 200 at Monteguillo in Jerez Superior in a single parcel and the other 100 in Sanlúcar de Barrameda and Chipiona. Those at Chipiona survived the phylloxera epidemic of the late nineteenth century and what is still known as Palomino de Chipiona was taken from them and grafted on to American plants to restock the whole Jerez region. Caballero owns five bodegas, those of San Francisco and the historic seventeenth-century San Bartolomé in Puerto de Santa María house 15,000 and 5,000 butts, and others in Jerez de la Frontera a further 4,000. The equipment has been thoroughly modernised, and the grapes are pressed at the vineyards to avoid damage during transport to the bodegas.

With agents and distributors worldwide, the firm is now one of the ten largest in the Jerez region and also owns a subsidiary, Vimanco, engaged in the export of La Mancha table wines, including the big-selling 'Rocamar'. At home, Caballero is best-known for its *ponche* (see page 101), a liqueur and digestif prepared with a basis of young brandy, extracts of sweet and bitter oranges made from fresh concentrate, together with sugar, almond extract and vanilla. In its gleaming silvered bottles and helped by spreads on billboards up and down the country of a sultry, décolletée redhead, domestic sales, well ahead of all competitors, amounted to 1·2 million cases in 1986.

The Burdon and La Cuesta sherries are separately described. Those from Caballero include a classic dry 'Pavón' *fino*; a beautiful amber-coloured *oloroso*, fragrant, complex and long in finish; the nutty 'Tío Benito' *amontillado*; and the 'Benito' range of 'Pale Dry, *amontillado*, pale cream and cream sherries sold in the United Kingdom by the C.W.S. The *ponche* is available in Britain as 'Poncello'.

Duff Gordon & Co.
Fernán Caballero, 3, Puerto de Santa María.
The historic house of Duff Gordon, now a part of OSBORNE Y CIA, was founded by Sir James Duff, British Consul in Cádiz, who was born in Ayrshire in 1734. His original dealings in sherry were through the house of Haurie (see also PEDRO DOMECQ), some of whose stocks he later took over, and his first London agent was George Sandeman (see also SANDEMAN-COPRIMAR). In 1768 he entered into partnership with his nephew, William Gordon, making a covenant with him in the following terms;

> We, James Duff and William Gordon, in El Puerto de Santa Maria, in the year 1768, undertake to grow and make our wines and brandies with all the respect and care that the old processes demand and our customers throughout the world deserve. We bind in this decision our successors so that the firm of Duff Gordon may never produce a bottle that does not meet the strictest requirements.

By 1805 business had so increased that Gordon set up the agency of Gordon, Murphy in London to distribute the wines; for a time it also handled the marketing of the Haurie sherries, and both the famous Pedro Domecq Lembeye and John James Ruskin, father of the writer, were employees. Sir James Duff died at eighty-one in 1815, a few months after the Battle of Waterloo, and was buried at sea off Gibraltar. His nephew and heir, who now became Sir William Duff Gordon, survived him for only eight years. The sherry business went to his son, Cosmo Duff Gordon, but since he was not yet of age, it was largely run by a talented German manager, John Nicholas Böhl de Faber, who was responsible for the move from Cádiz to Puerto de Santa María. By this time, the wines had become extremely fashionable in aristocratic circles and among the illustrious names on the company's order books were: the Duke of Gloucester, the Prince Regent, the Marquess of Hertford and the American writer and diplomat, Washington Irving.

Washington Irving arrived in Puerto de Santa María in 1828 for an extended visit, during which he stayed in a mansion belonging to the Osborne family while he wrote his *Conquest of Granada*. (It is visible down a tree-lined avenue off the road from Jerez, but passed to a member of the family whose American wife spent little time there and whose daughter recently sold it to a development company. The inside of the house has since been gutted and the gardens remodelled as an open-air discothèque spanned by a huge metal gantry with psychedelic lights.)

Irving became close friends with Böhl de Faber and encouraged his daughter Cecilia in her early literary efforts – she later became a famous novelist under the pen-name of Fernán Caballero. Irving was a sherry-lover and ordered supplies from Duff Gordon for the American Legation in London and also for diplomatic and consular centres in the United States. He also took samples of sherry to Russia, which so pleased the Czar, father of the ill-fated Nicholas II, that Duff Gordon laid down a *solera* for him. (I have tasted this 'Oloroso Viejísimo del Czar' at Osborne. It contains a little PX and is dark in colour, with a deep maderised nose, intense fig-like flavour and more or less endless finish.)

As time went on, Cosmo Duff Gordon turned more and more for advice on the running of the firm to Thomas Osborne, who had married Böhl's daughter Aurora. In 1833 he became a partner, effectively running the firm after Böhl's death in 1836, as did his son, also Thomas Osborne, after him. After the death of Cosmo Duff Gordon in 1872, the family sold out their interests to the Osbornes.

Although wholly owned by OSBORNE, Duff Gordon retains its own bodegas and *soleras* in Puerto de Santa María and exports a very wide range of sherries and brandies to most of the countries in Western Europe and the Americas, and further afield to Asia and the Far East.

Best-known of the sherries are 'Fino Feria', 'El Cid Amontillado' and 'Santa María Cream'.

Gómez S.A., Miguel M.

Avda Libertad, s/n, Puerto de Santa María.

Founded in Cádiz in 1816, the firm has remained in the hands of the family ever since. It was appointed a supplier to the Royal Household by King Alfonso XIII, a title which it still retains. The firm owns vineyards around Jerez, but the grapes are pressed in Puerto de Santa María, to which the firm removed its bodegas and old *soleras* in 1969. The most important export market is the United Kingdom. The *fino*, dry *oloroso* and *amontillado* are labelled as 'Alameda', the medium wines and pale cream as Gómez, and the cream as 'Leonor'.

La Cuesta, Bodegas

P.O. Box 6, San Francisco, 32, Puerto de Santa María.

The firm was founded in Puerto de Santa María in 1849 by Don José de la Cuesta and Don Luís de la Cuesta subsequently took over the important business of John William Burdon, who died childless. The combined concern was bought by LUIS CABALLERO in 1932, which continues to market sherries under both labels.

The La Cuesta range comprises a 'Troubadour' pale dry *fino*, slightly smoothened to the British taste; a 'Troubadour' medium *amontillado*; and a light and mellow 'Troubadour' cream.

Osborne y Cia, S.A.

Fernán Caballero, 3, Puerto de Santa María.

Thomas Osborne Mann was born in Exeter in 1781 and came to Cádiz at the turn of the century to join the firm of Lonergan and White, billbrokers, importers and exporters. The young man was befriended by Sir James Duff, the seventy-year-old British Consul and head of the important firm of Duff Gordon. When he first began shipping sherry on his own account, he was allowed to store it in Duff Gordon's bodega, and the two firms were henceforth closely linked under the management of a German manager, John Nicholas Böhl de Faber, whose daughter, Aurora, Osborne married in 1825. After the death of Sir James Duff in 1815 and Sir William Duff Gordon eight years later, Thomas Osborne became increasingly involved in the affairs of Duff Gordon and was made his partner by Cosmo Duff Gordon in 1833. After Thomas Osborne's death, his son Thomas Osborne Böhl de Faber, though not as yet of age, in due course both became a partner in Duff Gordon and took over the management of the family business; he is remembered in Puerto de Santa María for constructing the bull-ring, one of the largest and finest in Spain. His brother, John Nicholas, served as a diplomat and received the hereditary title of Count Osborne at the hands of Pope Pius IX in 1869, being the first member of a sherry family to be so ennobled. The firms of Duff Gordon and Osborne were finally united after the death of Sir Cosmo Duff Gordon in 1872, when the Osbornes bought out the interests of the Duff Gordon family.

Apart from making sherry Osborne is the largest producer of spirits in Spain. Veterano brandy, as the great black silhouetted bulls by the roadside constantly remind one, is the biggest-selling brandy in Spain. The company owns the distillers Jonas Torres in La Mancha; makes the famous 'Anís del Mono' in Barcelona; and produces 'Rives' gin in a brand new plant outside Puerto de Santa María. It also owns Bodegas

Montecillo in the Rioja, makers of the excellent 'Cumbrero' wines, and port lodges in Oporto.

The vineyards in the Jerez area extend to some 360 hectares, and the main bodegas and administrative offices, hung with purple bougainvillaea and flanked by a wide avenue lined with acacias, are among the most handsome in Puerto de Santa María. The vinification plant of La Atalaya (so-called because it is on high ground outside the town with wide views) is a remarkable construction with a soaring cantilevered roof unsupported by pillars or arches. Its architect was created Marqués de Tarroja on the strength of the design (he also designed the revolutionary 'Tío Pepe' bodega for González Byass), and the building is listed as a National Monument. The vinification tanks are also original. Of epoxy-lined steel, they are horizontal rather than vertical, allowing for more air space above the must and so approximating more closely to the conditions inside a traditional wooden butt. They number 194 and their total capacity is 7·75 million litres. The brandy bodega of El Tiro is also outside the town; a long, low building set amongst lawns and faced by bronzes of bulls, its *soleras* house 10,000 butts of maturing spirit.

Of the sherries, 'Fino Quinta' is one of the best of its type, very dry and pale in colour with a greenish cast, pungent and with almond-like taste. 'Coquinero' – slang for an inhabitant of Puerto de Santa María – is a pale, dry *amontillado* with intense nutty flavour. The 'Bailén' *oloroso* is rich, aromatic with a touch of sweetness. There is also a sweeter '10 R.F.' *oloroso* and three sweet cream sherries, 'Moscatel Fruta', 'Pedro Ximénez 1827' and 'Osborne Cream'.

All the Osborne brandies are matured in *solera*. 'Veterano', one of the biggest selling, if not *the* biggest selling in Spain, is dark-coloured, mellow, somewhat caramelised and made by adding macerated fruits to the spirit. This is the Osborne style, very much to the Spanish taste. The company was the first to react to the growing market for brandies in the medium price range, of which 'Magno' is a good example. The firm's premium brandies are 'Independencia' and the light and elegant 'Gran Reserva Conde de Osborne', for which it commissioned Salvador Dali to design a label and white ceramic bottle, slumping as if under the weight of years.

Portalto, S.A.
P.O. Box 68, Postigo, 14, Puerto de Santa María.
Portalto ships a range of sherries under the labels of 'Portalto', 'Don Diego', 'Ward Brothers' and 'Sharps'.

Terry S.A., Fernando A. de

P.O. Box 30, Santísma Trinidad, 2 & 4, Puerto de Santa María.
The Terry family from Ireland settled in Spain during the sixteenth
century. Don Fernando de Terry y Brucet, born in Cádiz in 1783, was
one of those who organised the defence of the city during the
Peninsular War and there is a street named in his honour. In 1816 he
was maturing and holding stocks of wine in Cádiz and Puerto de Santa
María, and in 1883 Don Fernando de Terry y Carrera expanded into
making and shipping brandy and sherry.

The old bodegas in the centre of Puerto de Santa María with their
grey-green olive trees shimmering in the sunlight are among the most
charming in the place. The wine is vinified at a large modern plant on
the outskirts. In 1981 the family sold the firm, ostensibly to a Catalan
bank, but it later transpired that this was simply a front for RUMASA.
After the conglomerate's collapse, it remained in government hands
until 1985 when it was bought by Harveys of Bristol.

Terry is famous in Spain for two things: its horses and its brandy.
The stud for the sturdy white Cartujano horses typical of Andalucía
and Jerez in particular is at the extensive *finca* of San José adjoining
the new winery, and they are stabled in the old bodegas of John
William Burdon. It was with these horses, known as Lippizaners in
Austria, that the celebrated Spanish Riding School in Vienna was
founded, and for which they still stand at stud. Although Harvey's are
pledged to maintain the stud, it was for the brandy rather than the
horses that they bought the firm. Prior to the acquisition Harvey's had
no access to the immensely important brandy market in Spain, and
Terry 'Centenario', smooth and with a touch of sweetness, sold in a
bottle with a distinctive yellow net, is one of the most popular in the
country. The older *reserva* '1900', *gran reserva* 'Imperio' and *reserva
especial* 'Terry I' are brandies of elegance and finesse.

Terry also makes a 'Maruja' *fino* sherry, light, dry and clean in the
style of Puerto de Santa María, and a soft 'Amoroso' with fragrant PX
nose. The lion's share of production, some 300,000 cases annually,
goes to Marks and Spencer.

Sanlúcar de Barrameda

Argueso, S.A., Herederos de
Mar, 8, Sanlúcar de Barrameda.
The house was founded in 1822 by Don León Argueso Argueso and possesses its own vineyards and *soleras*, but now belongs to A.R. VALDESPINO. It makes 'Pasada San León' and 'Extra' *manzanillas*, Argueso dry *oloroso* and *amontillado*, and a 'Moscatel Fruta' cream.

Argueso, S.A. Manuel de
P.O. Box 6, Jerez de la Frontera and P.O. Box 27, Sanlúcar de Barrameda.
Don León de Argueso, a wealthy farmer who had settled in Sanlúcar de Barrameda, founded the firm in 1822 and came to be one of the leading *almacenistas* with large stocks of the fine sherry. Towards the middle of the nineteenth century the firm acquired the bodegas of the well-known Gutierrez Hermanos in Jerez.

Of a complete range of sherries and brandies, it considers the finest to be its 'Señorita' *manzanilla*, grown in the area and made in the Sanlúcar bodegas, its 'Amontillado del Teatro' and 'Cream of Cream'. Its 'Manzanilla Pasada de Sanlúcar', one of the *almacenista* wines shipped by LUSTAU, is big and pungent with typically salty flavour and bitter almond finish.

52 The bodegas of Pérez Marin in Sanlúcar de Barrameda

Barbadillo, S.A., Antonio

P.O. Box 25, Luis de Eguilaz, 11, Sanlúcar de Barrameda.

Barbadillo, much the largest of the *manzanilla* firms, was founded in 1821 by Don Benigno Barbadillo y Ortiguela from the province of Burgos in Northern Spain. It remains in the hands of the fifth generation of this now Andalucían family. Its present head, Don Antonio Barbadillo, is also President of the Consejo Regulador for Jerez, and his father Don Manuel, whose recent death at the age of ninety-six was mourned by the whole of Jerez, was not only the leading authority on *manzanilla* but a gifted poet and novelist with some fifty books to his credit. These he wrote between six and nine in the morning in a study reserved for literary endeavour, before moving to a separate room to conduct the affairs of the firm.

The offices are in the former bishop's palace, and the complex of sixteen bodegas – of which even the Bodega Nueva ('new cellar') dates from before 1850 – are situated around the church of Santa María de la O and the tawny Moorish castle of Santiago in the centre of the town – hence the saying that the cellars are not in the castle, but the castle in the cellars. They are interspersed with secret green patios and walkways lined with acacia or rows of wine butts, and under the floors of the bodegas are cool cisterns for storing wine. There is a story of one of these that a worker tripped and fell through the manhole; he was flung a rope, but refused it, saying: 'No – just bring me some *jamón serrano*!'. In the manner of Sanlúcar, the *soleras* may contain as many as nineteen 'scales', and between them the different bodegas house some 60,000 butts.

Barbadillo owns important vineyards in Balbaina, Carrascal, Campiz and San Julián, and in partnership with HARVEYS has developed 1,000 hectares of new vineyards at Gibalbín, north of Jerez, together with one of the most modern vinification plants in the Jerez area. This is equipped with modern continuous presses of the latest type and temperature-controlled stainless steel fermentation tanks.

Apart from the wines made by INFANTES DE ORLEANS-BORBON, of which it owns 50 per cent, the firm produces a huge range of some sixty *manzanillas* and sherries under such names as 'Eva', 'Don Benigno', 'Viña de Cuco', 'King's Gold' and 'Embassy'. Among the best are:

Barbadillo *manzanilla fina*. Matured for the minimum of four years, this is pale, fragrant, bone dry and salty.

'Solear' *manzanilla pasada*. Despite the 24 years which is spends in *solera*, this is still light and fresh with all of Sanlúcar's salt breezes in the nose, a flavour of bitter almonds and a long, deep finish.

'Eva' *manzanilla*. 8 to 10 years in *solera* this is intermediate in style between the two previous wines.

'Principe'. A particularly fine *amontillado* with nuttiness, depth and long finish.

Barbadillo *oloroso*. Aged for 15 to 20 years, even in its fourth with fifteen to go, tasted from the butt this had lovely, fragrant nose, a good middle, and long, long finish.

Barbadillo P X. With an *helado de pasas al Pedro Ximénez* (ice cream with raisins) at Bigote's restaurant in Sanlúcar (see p. 111) this was sheer perfection.

'Fañez de Minaja' brandy. Old, in very limited supply, light mahogany in colour, of 40° strength, this is a beautiful oaky and mellow spirit with very long finish.

As well as sherries and brandies, Barbadillo also produces a fresh young 'Castillo de Diego' dry white wine, made from Palomino grapes, the first and best of its type, which should be drunk chilled and as young as possible.

C.A.Y.D.S.A.
P.O. Box 102, Avenida del Puerto, Sanlúcar de Barrameda.

The enterprise was founded in 1804 by a Genoese, Esteban Bozzano. After his death the name of the firm was changed to Viuda [widow] de Esteban Bozzano and in 1969 it was sold to a consortium of small firms, but was soon taken over by the main supplier of the wines, the Cooperativa del Campo Virgen de la Caridad. There are at the moment some thousand *socios* or members, many of whom own small vineyards.

The wine is fermented in a battery of earthenware *tinajas* of the type used in Montilla-Moriles (they are in fact stamped with the name of the maker in Montilla – the method is, incidentally, more common in the Jerez region than might be supposed; it has also been used by Garvey and Sandeman). To prevent the temperature of fermentation rising above 30°C, sulphur is sometimes added to the must, and this shows up in the nose and taste of some of the younger wines. The wines are matured in the usual way, and there are some 30,000 butts in the cooperative's *soleras*.

The co-operative makes and exports a full range of sherries, of which the best-known are the fresh young 'Bajo de Guía' *manzanilla* and rounder, more mature 'Manzanilla la Sanluqueña'; a pale, dry 'Cayd fino'; and a sweet 'Cayd Cream'.

Delgado Zuleta, S.A.

P.O. Box 4, Carmen, 32, Sanlúcar de Barrameda.

The archives of this prestigious firm establish that it was founded in 1719 by Don Francisco Gil de Ledesma, a Knight of the Order of Calatrava and Honorary Mayor of Sanlúcar. Over the years and with changes in the family, it went under various names before taking that of Don José Delgado Zuleta at the end of the nineteenth century.

Don José became a supplier to the Royal Household, and there is a picturesque story that King Alfonso XIII toasted the crew of one of his submarines with 'La Goya' *manzanilla*, while it was submerged in the Bay of Santander.

'La Goya', a first-rate and very fragrant *manzanilla pasada*, is the best-known of the trio made by the firm; the others are 'La Galvana' and 'Lola'. The other wines comprise a range labelled as 'Zuleta' and a good, dry and very clean 'Don Tomas' *fino*. There is also a *gran reserva* 'Monteagudo' brandy.

Infantes de Orleans-Borbón S.A., Bodegas

Baños, 1, Sanlúcar de Barrameda.

In 1886, Don Antonio de Orleans, Duke of Montpensier, decided to convert his 220-hectare sporting estate into vineyards. It was, however, only in 1943 that the Bodegas were founded; the *soleras* now run to 8,000 butts. Marketing of the wines is carried out by BARBADILLO, which now owns a 50 per cent share in the firm.

Best known of its sherries are the 'Torre Breva' *manzanilla*, 'Alvaro' *fino* and 'Orleans 1884 Cream'.

Medina y Cia, S.A., José

Banda de la Playa, 46, 48 and 50, Sanlúcar de Barrameda.

This family-owned company is of fairly recent origin and was formed by the acquisition of various bodegas in Sanlúcar de Barrameda and Jerez de la Frontera. It owns the Dos Mercedes vineyard of 107 hectares in the Carrascal region of Jerez Superior and by the purchase of the companies of B.M. LAGOS, LUIS PAEZ and JUAN V. VERGARA in Jerez, and HIJOS DE A. PEREZ MEGIA in Sanlúcar de Barrameda, holding some 30,000 butts between them, it has become one of the ten largest sherry companies. It is a major exporter to Europe, especially to the Low Countries, where it works with Heineken.

Medina is particularly well-known for its *manzanillas*, of which there are three: 'Medina', 'Medina Especial' and 'Solera 54'. It also markets a complete range of sherries with these labels and a 'Reserva Medina' brandy.

Otaolaurruchi, S.A., Carlos de

P.O. Box 300, Crtra Madrid–Cádiz, km 641·7, Jerez.

Started by a Sanluqueño in 1885, the firm was one of those to be engulfed by RUMASA and incorporated in BODEGAS INTERNACIONALES. Under its new management Internacionales continues to market Otaolaurruchi wines, both at home and abroad, especially in West Germany. The best-known is 'Manzanilla Victoria'.

Parra Guerrero, A.

P.O. 501, Jerez & Avenida Huelva, s/n, Sanlúcar de Barrameda.

Don Atanasio Guerrero Romero was distilling wine as long ago as 1794. The business was inherited by his daughter and handed down to his great grandson Antonio Parra Guerrero. For a time it was associated with the historic firm of J.M. RIVERO, the oldest in the sherry trade. It markets a range of sherries under own labels, such as 'Patrimonio' *fino*, 'Rey Sol' *oloroso*, 'Los Mellizos' *amontillado*, 'India' cream and 'Reconquista' brandy.

Pérez Marin, S.A., Hijos de R.

Banda Playa, 28, 11540 Sanlúcar de Barrameda.

This small bodega on the sea front, which makes one of the best *manzanillas pasadas*, 'La Guita', was founded by Don Domingo Pérez Marin in 1850 and has remained in the family until very recently, when it was taken over by a small consortium.

The bodega owns its own vineyards supplying the wine for the 'La Guita' *solera*, which runs to 2,000 butts, some of them more than a hundred years old, and with eleven scales. It spends some dozen years in the *solera* and emerges yellowish green, soft, extremely fragrant, salty and very dry. 'Guita' is slang for cash in Andalucía, and the story goes that the wine is so-named because Don Domingo would never part with a drop without payment on the nail. Apart from its slang meaning, *'guita'* also means 'twine' or 'string', hence the very individual presentation of 'La Guita', incorporating a string under its capsule, neck label and front label.

The other speciality is a *vinagre de yema*, one of the best of all sherry vinegars, made in *solera*, greenish-gold in colour and of quite astonishing fragrance and fruitiness.

Pérez Megía S.A., Hijos de A.

P.O. Box 21, Fariñas, 60, Sanlúcar de Barrameda.

Dating from 1821, the firm was in the fifth generation of the family which founded it when it was recently bought by JOSE MEDINA. It

makes a complete range of sherries, of which 'Alegría' is one of the
leading *manzanillas*, and 'Jalifa' a top quality *amontillado* made in the
soleras laid down by the founder.

Romero S.A., Pedro

Trasbolsa, 60, Sanlúcar de Barrameda.
The founder of the firm, in 1860, was Don Vicente Romero Carranza.
It is now associated with ANTONIO BARBADILLO and makes an
'Aurora' *manzanilla*, a complete range of 'Viña el Alamo' sherries, and
five different brandies.

Vinícola Hidalgo y Cia, S.A.

Banda Playa, 24, Sanlúcar de Barrameda.
Established in 1792, this is a family concern with 200 hectares of
vineyards in the Balbaina and Miraflores areas of Jerez Superior
sufficient to supply its needs and bodegas next to those of Pérez Marín
on the seafront at Sanlúcar. Their *soleras* run to 6,000 butts, and the
main brands are the famous 'La Gitana' *manzanilla fina* (all the best
manzanillas have feminine names), light, graceful and delicate with a
little apple in the nose; a good *manzanilla pasada* with a long, salty
finish; 'Jerez Cortado' and 'Napoleón *amontillado*, clean, smooth and
elegant, with overtones of dried fruit in the nose and a very long
finish.

Appendix

PRODUCTION AND EXPORTS OF SHERRY

STOCKS OF MATURING WINE AS OF 1 SEPTEMBER 1987

Bodegas de Crianza y Expedición

Jerez de la Frontera	3,414,854 hl.
Puerto de Santa María	485,357 hl.
Sanlúcar de Barrameda	572,656 hl.

Bodegas de Crianza y Almacenado

Jerez de la Frontera	108,108 hl.
Puerto de Santa María	17,992 hl.
Sanlúcar de Barrameda	113,992 hl.

TOTAL   4,712,960 Hl.

Register of Bodegas

Bodegas de Elaboración	108
Bodegas de Producción	37
Bodegas de Crianza y Almacenado	57
Bodegas de Crianza y Expedición	64

EXPORTS OF SHERRY

The following table and diagrams give a fairly complete picture of current sherry exports and of the trend over the last ten years.

Britain was for centuries by far the largest consumer of sherry and still accounts for almost fifty per cent of exports. Sales have, however, been falling since they peaked in 1979, the main reasons being a general fall in the sales of fortified wines in favour of greatly increased sales of light wines and competition from other drinks for the interest of the younger consumer. In a review of the sherry market in its issue of 14 April 1988, *Off License News* points out that the decline is smallest in the AB consumer group and considers that price is an important factor (hence the large sales of British sherry among the unsophisticated; wine writers, on the other hand, point out that for a wine of its quality sherry is *under*-priced).

The other northern European countries, notably Holland, Germany and Belgium, are importing an increasingly larger share. Exports to the United States remain very modest. The reasons for this have been well put in an article by Gerry Dawes in *The New York Wine Cellar* for 18 February 1988:

> American wine lovers get few opportunities to experience sherry at its best. Most retail outlets offer a few, often tired finos; several advertised brands of ersatz amontillados and olorosos (frequently not identified by type); an assortment of oversweetened creams, so-called cocktail sherries, and cheaper shippers' brands whose best application is for cooking; and, of course, the oxymoronic American sherries.
>
> The wine buff and would-be sherry aficionado will fare worse in restaurants, including the best wine bars. Even in establishments that have acquired a certain expertise in the handling of Champagne and Port, for instance, there is a woeful lack of knowledge about sherry, its storage, and its service, including proper glassware and correct serving temperatures. Such circumstances perpetuate low demand, virtually guaranteeing that hardly anyone will acquire a taste for sherry via the restaurant route . . .

Mr Dawes blames this unhappy situation on a variety of factors, including a failure of the producers to label their sherries clearly as *fino*, *amontillado*, *oloroso* etc. or to offer on the label any description of the style or indication of the degree of sweetness. He does, however, report that the enthusiastic reception of the *almacenista* sherries from Lustau in New York and on the Eastern seaboard is stimulating a revival of interest in sherry generally.

Exports of sherry 1987 (in hectolitres)

Country	Bulk	Bottled	Total
Andorra		1,301·43	1,301·43
Austria	2,043·00	1,172·00	3,215·00
Belgium	20,717·94	20,634·11	41,352·05
Canada	2,545·76	4,935·61	7,481·37
Denmark	7,576·70	11,622·35	19,199·05
Dominican R.	1,205·00	13·50	1,218·50
Finland	2,030·00	1,755·24	3,785·24
France	386·60	1,503·02	1,889·62
Holland	118,759·79	163,466·85	282,226·64
Ireland	2,857·28	4,316·84	7,174·12
Italy		1,109·61	1,109·61
Japan	13·71	2,905·46	2,919·17
Norway	3,679·00	1,058·56	4,737·56
Surinam & Dutch Antilles	25·00	1,860·54	1,885·54
Sweden	6,040·82	5,286·75	11,327·57
Switzerland	1,448·00	1,533·46	2,981·46
UK	265,462·67	111,055·43	376,518·10
USA		49,959·65	49,959·65
Venezuela	2,510·10	1,251·00	3,761·10
W. Germany	4,018·16	161,843·84	165,862·00
Others	406·98	15,816·77	16,222·75
TOTALS	441,725·51	564,402·02	1,006,127·53

Exports 1978 to 1987 (in 1,000 hectolitres)

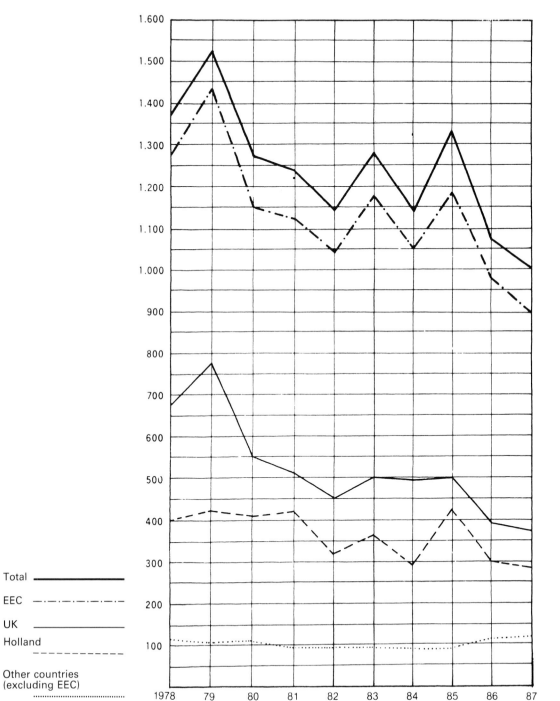

Total

EEC

UK

Holland

Other countries
(excluding EEC)

Exports 1978 to 1987 (percentage of market)

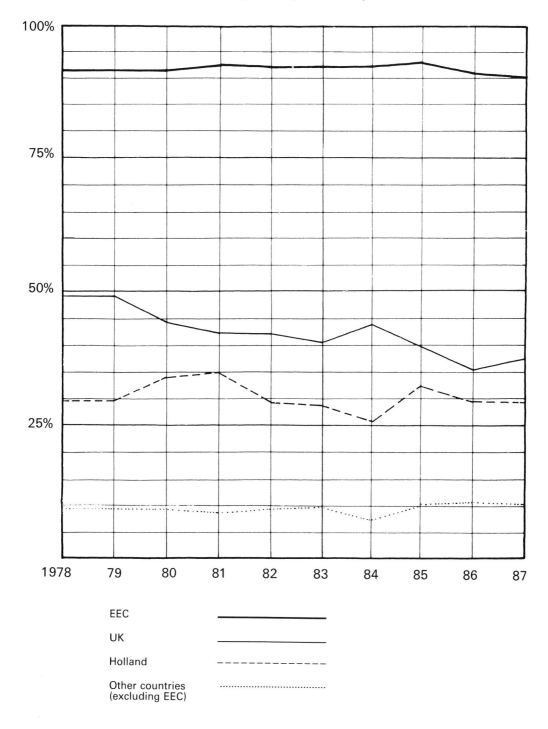

EEC	────────	
UK	────────	
Holland	────────	
Other countries (excluding EEC)	··················	

Glossary of wine terms

ABOCADO Semi-sweet.

AGUARDIENTE Grape spirit.

ALAMBIQUE A still.

ALBARIZA The best type of soil, white in colour and high in chalk.

ALMACENISTA A stockholder who sells wines to the shippers.

ALMIBAR A solution of invert sugar used for sweetening some pale sherries.

ALQUITARA A simple pot still producing grape spirit high in congeners.

AMONTILLADO A style of sherry, amber-coloured and with nutty flavour, made by ageing FINO.

AMOROSO A type of sweetened OLOROSO now usually described as CREAM.

ANDANA A tiered row of butts belonging to a SOLERA.

AÑADA Wine of a single vintage.

ARANZADA A measure of area equal to 0·475 hectares or 1·375 acres used for the vineyards.

ARENA A sandy soil, not of the best for viticulture.

ARROBA A measure of volume equal to 16·66 litres.

ARROPE A syrup used for sweetening wine and made by boiling down must.

ARRUMBADOR A workman in a sherry bodega.

BARRO A mainly clay soil ranked second in order of merit for growing sherry grapes.

BIENTEVEO A look-out tower in the vineyards for keeping watch on intruders at harvest time.

BOCOY A large butt, usually holding 40 ARROBAS or 666 litres and generally used for transporting wine.

BODEGA The lofty building above ground in which sherry is matured. The word is also used more generally in the plural of the whole establishment of a firm making and/or shipping sherry.

BOTA A butt. Made of American oak, the butts used for maturing sherry in the bodega hold from 600 to 650 litres. The smaller BOTA CHICA or shipping butt holds 500 litres.

CABACEO The blending or blend of wine.

CAMERA An open-sided wooden box containing a candle for assessing the limpidity of wines.

CANOA A large funnel with wedge-shaped container and a spout used in transferring wine from one butt to another.

CAPATAZ The head cellar man in a bodega, who keeps a constant check on the wines by tasting the contents of the butts and is also in charge of the workmen.

CASCO A single BODEGA under one roof in an establishment comprising several.

CEPA A vine

COLOR see VINO DE COLOR.

COÑAC The colloquial word for Spanish brandy.

CONSEJO REGULADOR The official organisation responsible for enforcing the regulations covering wines with DENOMINACION DE ORIGEN and controlling the quality, commercialisation and export of sherry.

COSECHERO An individual grower.

CREAM A dessert sherry, usually a sweetened OLOROSO, dark, fragrant and smooth. See also PALE CREAM

CRIADERA A 'scale' or series of butts containing wine of the same age, which is with withdrawn at intervals to 'refresh' another butt during the process of fractional blending.

CRIANZA The process of maturing a wine from the time that it is racked from the lees.

DEGUSTACION Tasting.

DENOMINACION DE ORIGEN The demarcation of a wine or spirit from an officially recognised region, corresponding to the French *Appellation d'Origine.*

DUELA A barrel stave.

DULCE Sweet.

DULCE APAGADO A sweet wine made by adding alcohol to unfermented must.

ELABORACION The making and further treatment of wine.

ENTRE-FINO A FINO sherry lacking distinction.

FINO A pale, light and dry style of sherry matured beneath a protective layer of FLOR.

FLOR A layer of yeasts growing on the surface of sherry while maturing in the butt. It is thickest in the case of FINOS and MANZANILLAS.

GARCETA A closely woven hemp sack, used in Sanlúcar de Barrameda when transferring wine from one butt to another to avoid disturbing the FLOR.

HECHO literally 'made'. Used of wines that are fully mature.

HECTAREA (HA) A hectare of 2·471 acres.

HECTOLITRO (HL) A hectolitre of 22 gallons.

HOGSHEAD A cask holding 245 litres or 54 gallons.

HOLANDAS Grape spirit containing some 60–70 per cent of alcohol and used for making Jerez brandy.

INJERTO A graft.

JARRA A jar used for transferring wine from butt to butt during TRASIEGO.

LAGAR An old-fashioned wooden winepress.

LEVANTE The parching, seasonal east wind.

LIAS The lees or solid matter deposited from newly-made wine.

LISTAN A synonym for the PALOMINO grape.

MANZANILLA The distinctive style of sherry made in Sanlúcar de Barrameda.

MEDIUM An AMONTILLADO or *amontillado*-type sherry or an OLOROSO which has been a little sweetened.

MISTELA A sweet must in which fermentation has been arrested by the addition of alcohol.

MITAD Y MITAD (or MITEADO) A 50/50 mixture of alcohol and sherry used for fortification.

MOSCATEL The well-known grape grown in the sherry region for making sweet wines.

MOSTO Must or freshly pressed grape juice. In Jerez it continues to be called 'must' after tumultous fermentation and until the new wine is racked from the lees.

OIDIUM A fungoid disease of the vine.

OLOROSO A dark, full and fragrant style of sherry matured without the presence of FLOR.

PAGOS A contiguous group of vineyards with similar characteristics.

PAJARETE, PAXARETE A dark coloured and very sweet wine, made partly from PEDRO XIMENEZ and used for sweetening both sherry and, in small amount, whisky.

PALE CREAM A type of CREAM sherry, pale in colour and made by sweetening FINO or light AMONTILLADO.

PALMA CORTADO FINO bordering on AMONTILLADO

PALMAS FINOS of high quality, marked one, two, three or four *palmas* according to age.

PALO CORTADO A rather rare style of sherry with the nose of an AMONTILLADO and flavour of an OLOROSO.

PALOMINO The most widely grown of the sherry grapes. There are two sub-varieties: the traditional Palomino de Jerez and the Palomino fino.

PEDRO XIMENEZ A grape which is sunned to concentrate the sugars and used for making the best sweetening wine.

PESO An old-fashioned monetary unit equivalent to 3.75 pesetas still used in transactions over the buying and selling of must and wine.

PHYLLOXERA An insect parasite of the vine, which has necessitated widespread grafting of the fruit-bearing vines on to resistant American stocks.

PODA Pruning. The method used in Jerez is that of *vara y pulgar*, leaving one long shoot and a knob for the following year's growth.

PONIENTE The prevalent cool west wind from the Atlantic.

PRENSA A press; also used of the second quality 'press wine' not used for making sherry.

PUNZANTE A word often used to describe the bouquet of FINO sherry; literally 'pungent', it refers to the volatile and aromatic nose of the wine.

PX An abbreviation of PEDRO XIMENEZ.

RAYA 1. A term used in classifying musts. 2. A coarse type of OLOROSO.

REAL Like the PESO, this is an old-fashioned monetary unit still used in buying and selling wine. One real is equivalent to 25 centimos, a quarter of a peseta or a fifteenth of a peso.

REGLAMENTO The printed code defining the requirements for wines with DENOMINACION DE ORIGEN.

ROCIADOR A perforated tube used to introduce wine gently below the FLOR during ROCIO (or 'refreshment').

ROCIO The 'refreshment' of a butt of wine in a CRIADERA or SOLERA with younger wine from another butt.

SACA The amount of wine drawn off from the SOLERA for bottling or shipment.

SACRISTIA A part of the BODEGA where visitors are invited to taste the wines.

SECO Dry.

SOBRETABLA A term used to describe young wine which has been racked free of the lees and is ready to enter the CRIADERA.

SOCIO A member of cooperative winery, who takes his grapes to be vinified there.

SOLERA Used generally to describe the system of butts used for the fractional blending and maturation of sherry. Strictly, the word applies to the bottom row of butts from which wine is periodically drawn for shipment or bottling.

TAJO A word descriptive of each of the individual operations involved in 'running the scales' of a solera and the successive drawing of wine and 'refreshment' of the butts.

TENT A corruption of *tinto*. Tent was a reddish-brown wine formerly made at Rota on the coast, now the site of the great U.S. naval base.

TIERRA DE LEBRIJA, TIERRA DE VINO 'Spanish earth' used for fining (clarifying) wine.

TONEL A large storage barrel holding several butts.

TONELERO A cooper.

TRASIEGO The operation of changing wines from one butt to another.

UVA A grape.

VELO The surface layer of FLOR in a butt.

VENDIMIA Vintage.

VENENCIA An instrument used for drawing samples of wine from a butt without disturbing the flor and consisting of a small silver or stainless steel cup on a long whalebone handle, or in Sanlúcar de Barrameda of a split bamboo.

VENENCIADOR The user of a VENENCIA, often the CAPATAZ.

VID A vine.

VIEJO, VIEJISIMO Old, very old.

VIÑA A vineyard.

VINO Wine.

VINO DE COLOR A wine used for darkening sweet sherries.

YEMA Must of the first quality obtained without mechanical pressing.

YESO Gypsum (or calcium sulphate), lightly sprinkled on the grapes before they are pressed to improve the quality of the must.

ZAPATOS DE PISAR The traditional cowhide boots studded with nails once used for pressing the grapes in a LAGAR.

Bibliography

ALLEN, H. WARNER, *Sherry*, London, 1933
  Port and Sherry, London, 1952
  A History of Wine, London, 1961

ALONSO, JUAN CARLOS, *Guía del tapeo en Triana*, Seville (Excmo. Ayuntamiento de Sevilla), 1985

BAKER, G. A., AMERINE, M. A. and ROESSLER, E. B., *Theory and Application of Fractional Blending Systems*, California, 1952

BARBADILLO, MANUEL, *El vino de la alegría*, Jerez, 1951

BORREGO PLÁ, 'El comercio del vino y el Puerto de Santa María en la crisis del noventa y ocho', in Vol. 1 of *Jornadas de Andalucía y América*, Seville, 1986

CONSEJO REGULADOR, Jerez-Xérès-Sherry y Manzanilla-Sanlúcar de Barrameda, *Estadísticas, Año 1987*, Jerez, 1987
  Los vinos de Jerez, Jerez-Xérès-Sherry, Jerez, 1987

CROFT-COOKE, RUPERT, *Sherry*, London, 1955

CUEVAS, JOSÉ Y JESÚS DE LA, *Vida y milagros del vino de Jerez*, Jerez, 1979

CUEVAS, JOSÉ, JESÚS Y JOSÉ MA., *Garvey Jerez, 1780–1980*, Jerez, 1980

DELGADO Y ORELLANA, JOSÉ ANTONIO, *La casa de Domecq d'Usquain*, Sevilla, 1966

DOMECQ, BELTRÁN, *Ageing of Sherry under Flor*, paper delivered at the International Symposium on Viticulture, Vinification and the Treatment and Handling of Wine, Oxford, 1982

FIFIELD, WILLIAM, *The Sherry Royalty*, Jerez, 1978

FORD, RICHARD, *A Handbook for Travellers in Spain*, London, 1845
  Gatherings from Spain, London, 1846

GONZÁLEZ, BYASS & CO. LTD, *Old Sherry*, London, 1935

GONZÁLEZ GORDON, MANUEL MA., *Sherry, the Noble Wine*, London, 1972

HENRY, THOMAS, *Harveys of Bristol*, Bristol, 1986

JEFFS, JULIAN, *Sherry*, 3rd ed., London, 1982

LUSTAU JEREZ (comp. Rafael Balao), *Guide to Sherry*, Jerez, 1979

MACPHERSON, LALO GROSSO DE, *Cooking with Sherry* (trans. Maite Manjón), Madrid, 1983

MANJÓN, MAITE, *The Gastronomy of Spain and Portugal*, London, 1989

MARCILLA ARRAZOLA, J., *Tratado práctico de viticultura y enologia españolas*, Madrid (Vol. 1, *Viticultura*, 1963; Vol. 2, *Enologia*, 1967)

MESA GINETE, FRANCISCO DE, *Historia Sagrada y Política de Jerez de la Frontera*, Jerez, 1888

OSBORNE Y CIA., S.A., *Osborne Grupo de Empresas*, Jerez, n.d.

PARADA Y BARRETO DIEGO, *Noticias sobre la historia y comercio vinatero de Jerez de la Frontera*, Jerez, 1868
Hombres ilustres de la Ciudad de Jerez de la Frontera, Jerez, 1875

PEMARTÍN, JULIÁN, *Diccionario del vino de Jerez*, Barcelona, 1965

QUIRÓS CARRASCO, JOSÉ MA., *Unas notas . . . sobre . . . yeso*, Jerez, 1958

RAINBIRD, GEORGE, *Sherry and the Wines of Spain*, London, 1966

READ, JAN, *The Wines of Spain*, London, 2nd ed., 1986
The Moors in Spain and Portugal, London, 1974

READ, JAN; MANJÓN, MAITE; and JOHNSON, HUGH, *The Wine and Food of Spain*, London, 1987

REDDING, CYRUS, *A History and Description of Modern Wines*, 3rd ed., London, 1851

ROXAS CLEMENTE, SIMON DE, *Ensayos sobre las variedades de la vid*, Madrid, 1807

RUMASA, *Rumasa 1961–1981*, Madrid, 1981

SANDEMAN SONS AND CO. LTD, GEORGE G., *The House of Sandeman*, London, 1979

THOMSON & CO., WM., *Ben Line Old East India Sherry, a Background History*, Edinburgh, n.d.

THUDICHUM, J. L. W., *A Treatise on Wines*, London, 1894

VIZETELLY, HENRY, *The Wines of the World, Characterized and Classed*, London, 1875
Facts about Sherry, London, 1876

YSASI, ENRIQUE DE, *Con una copa de Jerez*, Madrid, 1972

Illustration acknowledgements

I should like to thank the following for supplying photographs and for their permission to reproduce them in this book. Numbers are those of illustrations, colour plate references being in Roman numerals.

Consejo Regulador de la Denominación Jerez-Xérès-Sherry y Manzanilla-Sanlúcar de Barrameda: 14, 15, 27, 47, 49, II, VI

Croft Jerez, S.A.: 16, 26, 33, XIX

Diez-Mérito, S.A.: 45

Pedro Domecq, S.A.: 23, 24, III, VII, XIII, XV, XX

Gonzalez-Byass, S.A.: 36, 37, 38, 39, 40, 41, XVI, XVII

John Harvey & Sons (España) Ltd: frontispiece

Osborne y Cía: 13

Sandeman-Coprimar, S.A.: 12, 46, X, XII, XIV

Sherry Institute, London: 8, 9, 11

D. Enrique Ysasi Marenco: 5, V, VIII (reproduced in Enrique de Ysasi, *Con una copa de Jerez*, Madrid, 1972).

The remaining photographs were taken by the author.

The diagram on page 80 is reproduced by permission of Emilio Lustau, S.A., and those on pages 176 and 177 by courtesy of the Consejo Regulador de la Denominación Jerez-Xérès-Sherry y Manzanilla-Sanlúcar de Barrameda.

Index

Page numbers in *italics* refer to illustrations;
Roman numerals refer to colour plate numbers